E.T.S.U. AT TEXARKANA LIBRARY

PERGAMON GENERAL PSYCHOLOGY SERIES

Editors: Arnold P. Goldstein, *Syracuse University*
Leonard Krasner, *SUNY, Stony Brook*

New Sources of Self

PGPS–23

New Sources of Self

T. R. YOUNG

Red Feather Institute
For Advanced Studies in Sociology

PERGAMON PRESS INC.

New York · Oxford · Canada · Sydney · Braunschweig

0342207

018257

PERGAMON PRESS INC.
Maxwell House, Fairview Park, Elmsford, N.Y. 10523

PERGAMON OF CANADA LTD.
207 Queen's Quay West, Toronto 117, Ontario

PERGAMON PRESS LTD.
Headington Hill Hall, Oxford

PERGAMON PRESS (AUST.) PTY. LTD.
Rushcutters Bay, Sydney, N.S.W.

VIEWEG & SOHN GmbH
Burgplatz 1, Braunschweig

Copyright © 1972. Pergamon Press Inc.
Library of Congress Catalog Card No. 73-140581

All Rights Reserved. No part of this publication may be reproduced, stored in a retrieval system or transmitted in any form, or by any means, electronic, mechanical, photo-copying, recording or otherwise, without prior permission of Pergamon Press, Inc.

Printed in the United States of America
08 016672 5

Contents

0342207

018257

Acknowledgments

In the first instance, I am indebted to the many students in my class, "Individual in Society", who demanded more of me than establishment sociology. I also wish to acknowledge the support of Ann and Tim Lehmann who read the manuscript in the first draft and saw something of merit at that stage.

Robert Baker, whom I regard as harbinger of the new generation of professors, was kind enough to be critical. Joan Jensen, Peg Laswell and Sherrie Goss were especially helpful in all those ways known to every author. Jeanne Boland assisted in a variety of capacities which carried us through to completion. Charles Brown and David Schnell contributed ideas, insight, and data. I view Jeanne Boland, Charles Brown, and David Schnell as colleagues in this volume.

On behalf of the people who assisted me, I dedicate this book to the readers' children and to mine.

Foreword

In *The House of The Dead*, Dostoyevsky gives us a glimpse of the men whose self-structure neither grows from nor is lodged in the social order—men who act on impulse who are "self-willed". These men, forerunners of modern man, were torn by military conscription and by industrial changes from their ancient tribal identities (Lezghis, Tchetchenian, Daghestan, Great and Little Russians, and many more), left to fend for themselves, and to live for themselves. Whatever the magnitude of the problem in the time of Dostoyevsky, the problem has reached disaster proportions in our time.

It is critically important that we understand the self—its origins, its functions, its development and its expression. I do not believe there is a viable alternative to the self as the primary control unit of the psychobiological capacities of individuals. Power systems, penal systems, reward systems are of limited efficiency in constraining the behavior of masses of people taken one at a time. The self is superior as a source of order to a police state by quite some bit. Any society wishing to harness the capacities of its population in human and creative ways and toward humane ends must encourage the genesis and expression of self: more than that, the development of self must be mandatory. Societies with alternatives to self as the structural supports of large-scale systems must provide alternatives to selfhood. The underground church, the freak community, the zodiac, existential psychology, women's liberation, black power, encounter groups, and the free university are pioneer efforts in offering new sources of self and should be understood as such. Repression of these experiments means repression of self and is a greater tragedy than over-population, environmental pollution, and war itself.

At some point one must begin to realize that the separation of self from society, especially separation from large-scale organizations, is something short of a tragedy. I had been persuaded by the ideas of Cooley, the evidence

ix

of Mead, and the arguments of Marx that man's fate was tied to the social order and that separation should be reversed; now I am of the opposite conclusion. We must wean ourselves from society (from using preconstructed *social* models of self) just as we weaned ourselves from clan and soil in changing from peasant society to industrial society. The next generation of psychiatrists, clinical psychologists, and psychiatric social workers will "help" us to be unattached rather than adjusted to the social order. Perhaps, as self becomes separated from most of society, we can avoid the trade-off of alienation for affluence. Perhaps, if the case is made well enough in the pages of this book to a generation of social psychologists and sociologists, they, in turn, can help people live with themselves and for themselves . . . for without the self, society is pointless.

One thing more: as much as it is necessary to understand and encourage the development of the self, it is just as important to apply the principles of cybernetics to the constraint of large-scale organizations. It is in this area where the real chaos and savagery exist. Most individuals have some semblance of self as a control component, even if fragmentary, and this self reflects to some extent values which advance the human condition. The same cannot be said of large-scale establishments. That this book focuses upon the individual does not mean that I am unappreciative of the need for social control of the military, of commerce, of business. I agree with Fromm that technology must be humanized at that level of systems organization and operation. And since Fromm has said that before and said it better, I want to focus on the importance of the self as crucial to the domestic tranquility as well as the human condition as a means to advance the work of Fromm.

Redfeather, Colorado   T. R. YOUNG

CHAPTER 1

Introduction

Modern society has become much too flimsy a fabric out of which to build a self-system. Coming to understand this, I was forced to reexamine the social sources of self and to do that I had to return to Mead, Cooley, Piaget, Marx, Freud, Simmel, Baldwin, and many, many more. Rereading their arguments and evidence, I was even more impressed than during earlier readings. The evidence adduced by these analysts left little doubt that self developed out of the social order, was called forth during social encounters, and found its expression (or repression) in the social order. But, self could not be irrevocably linked to such a society as our contemporary one.* From the point of view of basic human needs, society is sick. From the point of view of modern business, things are improving.

The fact of the matter is that we have a considerable segment of society (large-scale organizations) which bears little or no relevance for one's own self. LSOs have become even more the typical unit of organization and experience in a complex society, leaving even less of the remainder of society from which to derive self and in which to express self. LSOs are becoming too formal, too predictable, too well-ordered, too planned for most of us who came into contact with them to generate and to express a multidimensional self. In a word, society is becoming too rational (in the sense of Tönnies) for a whole human to emerge and find sustenance. In large-scale establishments the assumptions as to the relationship between society and selfhood held by the symbolic interactionists simply do not apply.

The looking glass process does not occur; self is not the focus of interest; and the language used ceases to arouse those cognitive orientations, emotional orientations, and behavioral orientations central to the human condition.

---

*By "society," I mean *Gesellschaft* in its technical sense; formal, rational, impersonal society as distinct from Gemeinschaft—community.

1

There is language to be sure, but it is the language of commerce rather than the language of life. It is the language of the computer rather than the language of people. There are processes to be sure, but these processes are ahistorical, discontinuous, episodic forms focusing upon the task of making the large-scale system a going concern rather than making the self-system a going concern. These observations apply to one's experience in schools, churches, factories, offices, sports, businesses, stores, and agencies. One realizes that nowhere in the social order is self of central interest to the establishment; self is assumed. Police protect property rather than monitor behavior, or direct traffic, or investigate violence and "subversion." In spite of Dewey, in the schools classes are centered on subject matter rather than children. Mass media is mass communication, interested more in selling than being or becoming. One wonders where one can find components with which to construct a good and satisfying self in such a social order.

A central theme in this book is that the psychobiological capacities of individuals are in the process of being replaced in "modern" society by the electromagnetic capacities of technology, by the decision-making and control capacities of business systems, by the physical capacities of modern industrial machinery. There are several consequences of this replacement that need to be explored. In the first instance, great harm is done to the process by which the self-system is generated. As long as man can remember, the self-system was the repository and control center of those psychobiological capacities necessary to produce society in all of its aspects. For this reason, the process of creating a self-system for each person was given great and painstaking attention. Now the art and craft of system building does not focus upon the self but upon the large-scale organization and its included components. No longer does the fate of a social system hinge upon the fate of self-development, self-actualization, and self-expression; this linkage is too tenuous, too unpredictable, too cumbersome for modern business and industry. Rather than rely upon the adequacy of self-structure of any given set of individuals, modern organizations strive for stability by generating some one or few unit acts on the part of millions of customers through need, through persuasion, depth psychology, or deception by means of advertising strategies.

"Primitive" societies build their political, religious, military systems right into the self-system of a given number of trainees. This self-structure lasts the life of the individual and outlasts any given occasion for its expression. One is always a Catholic, a doctor, a policeman, father, or a tribesman.

Assuming the discontinuation of this historic linkage between self and social order, one wonders as to the need and the new sources, as well, of self. If the psychobiological capacities of people cease to be continuously useful to the "developed" societies, one wonders about the new sources of such capacities: love, passion, frivolity, shame, joy, sex, anger, skill, strength, craft, energy, interest, concentration, pain, satisfaction, hunger, sin, and contemplation.

To say that the capacities of man are replaced by alternative technologies is commonplace. What is important to understand is that the genesis and expression of these capacities has, heretofore, been tied to the genesis and expression of self. These capacities, enclosed in role assignments and expressed as social identities, constituted the core of self. Without such organization of capacities, without such social identities, self becomes a fragile affair.

Yet it is self which is the organizer of behavior; it is self which scans the situation and matches behavior to role in appropriate ways. It is self which functions as the control component of a complex cybernetic system by which behavior arises. It is essential to have self in order to contain and constrain one's own behavior. Without self, man is little more than a savage, roaming the streets and following whims and urgings with little reflection, little coherence, little unity: that unity comprises the individual as such.

Whatever large-scale organizations do and do well, they do not attend to the task of selfhood construction. Churches, schools, businesses, families cease to be simultaneously concerned with organizational goals and selfhood. Without the traditional supports of selfhood, a society must provide for alternative sources of self as well as alternative modes of expression of self, often at one and the same time.

In the pages which follow, I shall develop two points—one, that the task of socializing persons to possess social identities is irrational to mass society and, two, that even the psychobiological capacities of humans, whether controlled by the self-system or not, are becoming less useful to large-scale systems as other technologies for data control and for work become adopted.

I will then strain the credulity of the reader by providing an interpretation of some contemporary social movements as ventures in the private construction and private use of self. What I mean by this is that these settings—the freak community, the underground church, especially the free university, as well as encounter groups and hermitage among others—provide those persons involved with a wide range of values and lines of endeavor which each is able to assemble in a unique and private self-system to be used in private ways. Existential psychology and psychiatry are beginning to provide the means to do this while Maslow (1959) has provided the ideology of self-actualization.

The private construction and use of self is a revolutionary endeavor. It is made necessary by the principles of sound management, effective organization, good advertising, and creative leadership applied in business, finance, commerce, and industry originating in schools of business, institutes of technology, departments of economics, and colleges of engineering. It is the engineers, the managers, the systems analysts, the data control specialists who are godfather to the freak.

Once we understand the source and the essence of the social movements above, we have the basis for insightful response to them. We may choose to dismantle the progeny of modern capitalism and communism: mass society, LSOs, public bureaucracies, or we may choose to retain and humanize them after the ideas of Fromm (1968). If we do the latter, and that is as certain as a thing can be, then we must support, as a matter of public policy, private, individual responsibility for self-design, self-development, and self-actualization.

In the final pages of this book, I will provide the reader with some sense of what is involved in the private construction and private use of self. Much of what is involved is presently considered immoral and corrupt. And indeed it is immoral when the point of existence is to harness one's human capacities to production, to data control, to research, to transportation and such. With hardware alternatives, such social monopoly over the range of human abilities is less critical to those activities.

Norman O. Brown conveys a similar message: "Permanent revolution then, and no permanent structures issuing from contract, commitment, promise, will or will power, which are from the ego. Not voluntarism, but spontaneity, or grace; not the ego but the id" (in *Psychology Today*, August, 1970, p. 44). While one may (properly, I believe) question Brown's exegesis of alienation as stemming from an inability to affirm death, the fact of the matter is that Brown reaffirms life and, given a choice between Brown on the one side and a Kissinger on the other, there can be little doubt that wave after wave of the younger generation will opt for the Brownian movement: erotic, ecstatic, playful, poetic, and polymorphously perverse; there are loves stranger to the human condition than one's body.

Before moving into the heart of the matter, it is necessary to develop at length some points for those interested in the more technical aspects of my thesis concerning the separation of self and society. For these my colleagues, I have provided Chapters 2, 3, 4 and 5. Those who wish to focus upon the new sources of self and the private uses may want to skim the early chapters and read more closely the last two chapters.

CHAPTER 2

Self-structure and Social Structure

A REEXAMINATION

In this chapter, I would like to reexamine an old assumption; that self and society are twinborn. I wish to question the necessity of the social order being the primary source of "human nature." I do not want to reject society as an important contributor to self-structure: only to examine the ways in which self and society are linked and are separated.

I want social psychologists to rethink the way in which the self arises: not in challenging symbolic interactional theory (Mead, 1934; Blumer, 1969) but rather to ask if symbolic interaction does, indeed, occur in large-scale organizations, and, if so, does that symbolic interaction generate self-awareness and self-development as surely it did when Mead wrote; or whether the central focus of symbolic interaction in a large-scale organization is not, rather, put to quite different purposes other than organizing a self-system and sustaining it.

I want to challenge the Marxian assumption that separation of self from work produces alienation in contemporary society as surely it does in societies where self and society are twinborn. . . and where occupational social identities are close to the core of the self-system. Durkheim held that social facts produce individual facts; we may question, properly, whether, among the individual facts produced, the self-system is one such fact, as well as question the conditions under which this is true, partly true, or not at all true.

To what extent is self and society twinborn? In primary groups self is spun in complex ways; in secondary groups, there is little opportunity to reflect and less opportunity to reflect upon the self. What happens to the sources of self in a complex society where large-scale organizations cease to be an incidental aspect of the social order and begin to be a dominant aspect?

5

In what ways does it make sense to say that self and society are twinborn and how is this relationship ascertained? If we can measure the degree to which social order and self-order are coterminous, we can validate, refute, or revise Mead, Cooley, Rose, Blumer, and the rest. If self is not coterminous with society, then either self arises from some given subset only of the social order, or perhaps from nonsocial as well as social sources.

The Emergence of Self

There are three major ways in which it is proper to speak of self and society being twinborn: once in the emergence of self through the socialization process within primary groups, again in the presentation of self in everyday society, and once again in the fact that the core of self is comprised of a set of social identities which themselves derive from the social differentiations in society: occupational, sex, age, class, political, religious, and familial. Thus one is a farmer, a male, an adult, a Republican, a Presbyterian, as well as father, husband, son, and brother. The emergence of self in developmental phases has received excellent treatment by Mead, Cooley, Baldwin, Piaget, Blumer, Garfinkel and many others. Chapter 3 of this work presents in some detail the assumptions, arguments, and evidence attesting to the development of self out of the social order and by means of the social order.

Sherif and Sherif (1969) have presented us with an excellent up-to-date text which carefully sets forth the major principles that permit one to understand the complicated role society plays in generating a self-system *via* symbols used in social interaction. Few people have delved as deeply as Piaget (1962) into the element of play in enabling the child to differentiate a self from his surroundings. Garfinkel (1968) has forced us, against our will perhaps, to understand that any given component of the self requires a great deal of effort on the part of the person concerned to construct it.

In one of the most profound treatises written, Goffman assembles the evidence to unveil the routines of self-system generation, destruction, obliteration, and reordering which occur in asylums and other total institutions (1961). In following the moral (self) career of the "mental patient" the features of the social order; the whole round of life, records, conferences, clothing, degradation, privileges, permissiveness, and underlife as well as many other such features are connected by Goffman to the changes in the self-system of those caught up in those asylums and total institutions. If the development of self from social order is not made clear in Mead and Piaget, dealing with the young and innocent, it is established irrefutably by Goffman and Garfinkel in observing the shaping and reshuffling of self-systems of adults. In *Ethno-methodology* (1967), Garfinkel dissects a case history of a young person who must, largely alone, become a young lady. The fact of the matter is that the young person succeeds, but what is of importance to the social psychologist is that the details of this generation of self is available to study. Garfinkel gives us an account of the efforts made and the difficulties faced, as well as the technical solutions adopted in that endeavor.

But most socialization is more routine and, therefore, scarcely noticeable as such. In folk societies and, until recently, in complex societies, specific social identities anchored in the social order became lodged in the personality system of the specific individual through a socialization process, each process is different for each social identity, each set of social identities is different for each individual. By the time given persons have been cycled through the socialization process, cycled through a specific rites of passage, and "placed" in given social positions, they come to believe that they *are* one of the social identities in question. People come to believe that they *are* doctors, prostitutes, police, "Niggers," miners, bosses, and such similar social identities. This is one major way in which it is necessary to speak of self and social order as twinborn.

Most persons go through 5 to 15 such socialization routines and come to have from 5 to 15 social identities as the core of their self-system. These identities serve to organize behavior of persons across time and society in holistic, challenging, as well as in satisfying ways.

But after the psychological structures are organized and the self-system is adequate to its culture, the self still does not exist in any phenomenological sort of way until the definition of the situation requires the individual to put himself into situational harness, turn on his psychobiological capacities to perform the role for which he is equipped, and begin to be an *actor* in ways observable and with ways of consequence to the reality around him. It is in this area, the presentation of self after it is developed, that Goffman provides us with data, interpretation, and insight.

The Presentation of Self

Goffman (1959, 1961a, 1961b, 1963, 1967) provides us with the cold light of dispassionate scrutiny by which to reveal the manifold ways we daily use ourselves in order to generate social order. The ways we generate a specific definition of the situation in distinction to all other possible definitions of the situation are varied indeed, but this we do. Sometimes we use clothing to help us establish a definition; sometimes we use body tonus with face, leg, and eye discipline; sometimes we use emotional states; sometimes we use our capacity to define external and internal happenings as irrelevant—and the more distracting are these happenings: hunger, fatigue, personal problems, the more "self-control" we must have in order to successfully define them as irrelevant to the legitimate normative order. Goffman discusses all of this in precisely those terms.

We must, if there are to be certain kinds of social reality, allocate our intellectual, emotional, and behavioral capacities to the involvement: Is this a funeral, a party, a class, a game? Each requires that we strain our human capacities in that particular pattern and, when we do so, social reality is just as real as any other kind of reality one can name. And, when we cease to organize our behavior, our feelings, our intellectual capacities in ways compatible with the normative order, society is disassembled and exists no more. It is in this sense one can say, properly, that self and society are twinborn. Without our psychobiological capacities there would be no games, no classes, no art, no drama, no religious service.

Nor would there be any such thing as General Motors, The Catholic Church, Harvard, or the Masons if some of us, some of the time, did not manage our presentments, shield our delicts, sustain our involvements and, as well, define as irrelevant all of the physiological drives, psychological needs, social expectations, and cultural values which are incompatible with the legitimately given normative order.

For the most part, the elicitation of our psychobiological capacities requires a definition of the situation to be sustained, a normative order by which to pattern behavior, as well as the possession by the person in question of a legitimate presenting identity. These three factors—one cultural, one social, and one psychological—constitute a tripartite structural basis by which a given social occasion arises.

In a particular setting, a person develops considerable skill in reading the symbolic cues which identify a given definition of the situation, that of school, church, play, work, love, and so on. That person draws upon his recollection of past experiences as the bases for choosing among a wide variety of normative constellations with which he is familiar. At the same time, he is able to select among the 15 or so social identities just that one matching the social occasion. If all is well, a person is able to orchestrate these components to the mutual satisfaction of all concerned.

Should the definition of the situation be clouded, one spends a little time settling the question of what's going on. If the normative set should be in question, authority or prestige rankings are conventional ways to settle the issue. However, if one does not legitimately "possess" a presenting identity suitable to the occasion, one feels no need to match psychobiological capacities to the social order. Under the last condition, one is dismissed or one withdraws: physically if possible, sociologically if not.

In the concrete instance, a person may be invited to attend a religious service. If he arrives at the designated place at the designated time, he may find all the symbolic cues asseverating the "religious" character of the occasion: pews, aisles, stained windows, choir, quietude, and subdued decorum. The definition of the situation is clear and one has little doubt about either the structure of norms or about which society identity he is to bring to bear as a point of departure for organizing his own behavior.

If, as may happen, one attends "another" church, one knows the definition of the situation but may be in doubt about the norms. One may be provided with a bulletin by which to order one's behavior or may observe closely the pattern set by others present and very quickly follow suit. If the norms require great skill or some special knowledge, one may sit quietly. By doing so one has withdrawn sociologically.

If the person in question has not been subjected to socialization routines, he may not think of himself as a Catholic, as a Christian, as a Buddhist, or whatever social identity and, once again, withdraw.

All of the foregoing attests to the complexity of the process by which society emerges as a distinct reality, as well as the intimate relationship between self and social order in that process. It is fair to say that self and society have been twinborn for the better part of history. Social systems have depended upon the presentation of some social identity lodged in the self-system of the participants. People have drawn upon the social order for each and every identity of the several which constitute the heart of the self-system.

Both processes, the construction of self through the early years in primary groups and the presentation of self as self, are integral to understanding how psychobiological capacities are transferred from the separate individual to the social system. When both processes occur, one in the past and one in the present, then there *are* doctors, there *are* students, there *are* peasants. The social order emerges as a separate and new level of reality, the primary support of which is some component of the self system—a specific social identity.

All this is no small accomplishment; to find 60 healthy individuals ordering their behavior in ways compatible with one definition of the situation on any given day in any given place is an improbability of incalculable magnitude: for people to do such is testimony to their huge capacities as human beings. But, for large-scale organizations, human capacities are not enough; as predictable as human behavior is it is not predictable enough for professional system designers. For those who design transportation systems, human capacities are too imperfect; the toll taken on the highways attests to this. For those who design financial systems, human capacities to decode, store, retrieve, and encode information are too slow, too careless, too casual. All those magnificent capacities adequate to the task of generating love, worship, war, and art are being phased out by large-scale organizations in their search for order and stability beyond the touch of the second law of thermodynamics.

The central theme of this volume is that social structure takes a new relationship to self-structure in advanced *Gesellschaft*.* In these societies, self is generated in more private ways and maybe put to more private uses. In advanced *Gesellschaft* social systems obtain their own structure by means other than the self-system or by means of psychological states. This release of the self-structure by LSOs permits the individual to fashion a self composed list of items and elements not functional to making the social system go.

In the traditions, polemics, and theories of deviant behavior and social disorganization, there is the ubiquitous assumption that self without society yields alienation. In this monograph we will examine that assumption as well as the assumption that self arises from society, and put forth still another: that there is a continuing and progressive replacement of self by more "rational" structural supports for social systems encompassing greater and greater segments of the population. This view is markedly different from that which holds there is a separation between self and society that is tragic and must be reversed. The position I take is that the disaffiliation process is irreversible and that alienation is a temporary by-product. As man turns to new sources of self, he will emerge healthier, more autonomous, more an individual, and more human. In particular, I mean to say that as the amount of human behavior required to make complex institutions thrive decreases, more and more behavior of humans can be turned to the pursuit of human experiences: peace, ecstasy, anguish, loneliness, delight, even madness. If complex institutions are a hostile environment to the experience of self and if complex institutions are too important to discard, then it follows that new, noninstitutional sources of self must be sought.

In Chapter 3, I will review the manifold theoretical perspectives in which self is linked to society. In the second half of the chapter I will also try to concretize and simplify the idea that self and society are twinborn via the notion of "social identity," and I will offer an operational definition of self as well as suggest a methodology (after Kuhn, 1954) for gauging the degree of affiliation between self and society.

Next, I abstract from the symbolic interactionists the major mechanisms

---

*Formal, rational, impersonal society wherein the typical unit of experience is the large-scale organization.

by which self emerges from society so we can examine the social order of complex organizations to know if these mechanisms are operative. This concern links Chapter 3 with Chapter 5. In Chapter 4, 1 want to acknowledge and to question the tragic version that self, separated from society, produces alienation and conflict. Finally, I want to offer some new sources (Chapter 6) and some private uses (Chapter 7) of self which I see to be an alternative to the tragic view of self without society.

CHAPTER 3

Self-system: Delineation and Measurement*

THE CYBERNETICS OF SELF-CONTROL

There are many distinguished behavioral scientists who accept the notion of the "self" more as a matter of faith than of observation. In general, we will treat the self as though it exists. While I will present an operational approach to the delineation of the self-structure, at this point I should like to give it as understood that the self is a complex pattern of behavior rather than a physiological or psychological datum.

In this section, I shall briefly outline the way in which the self functions as the primary source of control (order) operating as a control component in a fairly complex cybernetic system. This is a greatly simplified paradigm, deliberately so in order to show the reader the points in similarity between the self in operation and the features of cybernetic control systems in general. I am most interested that the reader focus on the role of the self as an integral part of a real system rather than as an abstraction or as a disconnected construct.

If we understand the self as real and integral then we can understand the conditions under which it really exists or fails to exist. If, as I believe, the best source of order lies in individual exercise of selfness rather than in external controls, then it is obvious that industrial societies must reorder priorities assigning immediacy to the endeavor to produce self as against any commodity one could name or made do with police, manipulation, and other external controls.

In phenomenological terms, the self does not exist unless it is assembled and operates in the cybernetic configuration below inasmuch as the delineation of self presented here is as *patterns* of behavior. When that pattern is

*With the assistance of David Schnell.

lacking, the self is lacking, and that control deriving from the self is lacking. The general features of a cybernetic control system (after Buckley, 1967) include (a) a monitoring apparatus, (b) a set of parameters (or constrains), (c) an effector apparatus, and (d) a control apparatus by which to reduce mismatch between the performance of (c) and the implicit directives of (b). In the next paragraph, one is able to note the similarities in structure between cybernetics and self-control.

In practice, self-control involves the following *patterns* of behavior as minimal components: (a) monitoring behavior in which a person observes his own behavior and compares it with one of the following: (b_1) his recall of *his* responsibility for the normative structure (his social indentity) of a given social role, or (b_2) coherent expectations (roles) levied on him by role-other(s), or (b_3) various options which he is able to synthesize on the spot but which are compatible with (b_1) and (b_2) (role-making), and (c) adjustments in his own behavior by which to reduce mismatch between (a) and (b) above (self-control).

As you might note, there are three subsets of behavior above, two of which involve the individual in question and a third pattern which involves role-others directly (expectations) or indirectly (normative structure). This is a central meaning of the concept that society and self are twinborn. When these three components of the self exist as a system, I conceive it to be a social self. When (b) above involves neither role-others nor normative structures but rather, (b_4), (b_5) . . . (b_n), then I would prefer to speak of the private self in distinction to the social. (b_4), (b_5), . . . (b_n) are operationally defined as elements of the self-system which are not sponsored by any large-scale organization or coerced upon one by any social unit. But before one can begin to conceptualize the self in these terms, it is necessary to examine a prior question: what evidence is there that self is anchored in society and how is this relationship conceptualized? The review which follows attends to that interest.

THE SOCIOLOGICAL PERSPECTIVE

Karl Marx was among the first to be taken seriously in his insistence that self arose from society. The Marxian view is that self is a function of an individual's *position* within his society. In *Economic and Philosophical Manuscript* (1844) he declares:

> The individual is a social being. The manifestation of his life—even when it does not appear directly in the form of social manifestation, accomplished in association with other men—is therefore a manifestation and affirmation of social life. (cited in Bottomore, 1964, pp. 116–7)

For Marx, behavior, thought, perception, and consciousness all keyed off from the economic institution of an individual's society, and therefore the class to which the individual belonged. To change the self-system, the Marxian perspective would require a change in the social, especially the economic, system. After Marx, there could be little doubt as to the source of self. With Marx, the source of self became a political question. One major reason Marxists became so thoroughly proscribed lies in the fact that political means were used to settle what had before been a religious or academic issue. However, on this point, the Marxian perspective is correct. Many of the difficulties in the areas of self-control, self-expression, self-fulfillment arose from the intimate relationship between self and the social order. That the social order could be so cruel a component of self was a view which contradicted all the rhetoric of socialization: love of family, love of culture, love of country, morality of community, and sanctity of occupation. Law, religion, and morality created a consciousness false to selfhood and to life itself. This analysis assumes the inseparability of self from social order. I return to question the validity of this assumption in Chapter 5. However appropriate the assumption in 1850, and I believe it was, a real question exists about the assumption in 1971.

Durkheim, too, states that the self (he refers to it as individuality) is a product of tradition and community. Only in society can the individual be discovered and only through the behavior of the individual can society be known. "Collective life is not born from individual life, but it is, on the contrary, the second which is born of the first" (Durkheim, cited in Nisbet, 1965). Society as a whole, through the media of social facts and collective representations, forms the individual being. When removed from civilization, a man exists only on the level of sensation, for it is society that forces the individual to transcend his physiological self and provides him with the means to do so. Durkheim viewed society as greater than the individual, "going beyond him," but also entering him and everywhere being an aspect of man's nature. It is of interest to note that Durkheim felt that, as civilization became larger and more complex, the individual would feel smaller in relation to it and the amount of civilization that would be integrated into that individual would diminish. Less complex civilizations can be fully integrated into the individual whereas more complex ones cannot, a point to which I return again.

Durkheim distinguishes two components of one's "being" (read self). One part, the individual being, is composed of all the mental states which apply solely to the individual and the events of his personal life (my b_4, b_5, . . . b_n). The other part, the social being (social self), is composed of a system of ideas, sentiments, and practices which express in the individual, not his personality, but that of the group or groups of which he is a member (b_1, b_2 and b_3).

In *Human Nature and Social Order* (1902), Charles Horton Cooley developed the concept of the looking-glass self.

> The looking-glass self, the social self, arises reflectively in terms of reaction to the opinions of others on the self. A self idea of this sort seems to have three principal elements: the imagination of his judgment of that appearance, and some sort of self feelings, such as pride or mortification. (p. 159)

The looking-glass self arises through symbolic interaction between an individual and his primary group. The primary group is characterized by: (1) face-to-face association, (2) unspecified nature of association, (3) relative permanence, (4) small number of persons involved, and (5) the relative intimacy of the participants. In such a group, an intimate fusion of individuality and group exists. Such groups are primary in several senses, but chiefly in that they are fundamental in forming the social nature and ideals of the individual. The function of primary groups is to provide face-to-face relationships which produce feedback for the individual to evaluate and relate to his own person. The self is formed by a trial and error learning process through which new sets of values, role orientations, and social identities are acquired (Cooley, 1902; Martindale, 1960).

Building on and expanding Cooley's concepts, George Herbert Mead produced his theory of the development of self. Leaving no question as to the social origins of the self, he proposed that the self is not present at birth but must develop, emerging from the process of social activity and experience. Self develops in a given individual as a result of his relations to that process as a whole and to other individuals within that process (Mead, 1934).

The self is essentially a social structure, arising as it does from social experience. Once it has arisen, it can provide social experience for itself (my source for (b_1)). Thus, we can conceive of a solitary self but not of one originating outside of social experience. The self is composed of various elementary selves which answer to the various aspects of the structure of the social process. The structure of the complete self is thus a reflection of the entire social process. It is composed of all the elementary selves, each of which reflects on aspects of the social process, and the total collection of which reflects the entire social process to which the individual is exposed. When Mead wrote this analysis, it was, I believe, accurate for the vast majority. However, many social processes in complex systems no longer involve the self-components of persons in those processes even though those persons may be involved. The investiture of social identity in self-system is not a requirement in mass society . . . all that is required is that one allocate some behavior on some few and short occasions. Hetzler (1969) refers to this presentation of self-image for short periods as "drama of the mid-line." It is halfway between a theatrical performance in which one knows he is not the thing he portrays, and, on the other side, naïve performance in which one is certain that he has a self which matches the social process.*

According to Mead there are two stages in the full development of the self. The first stage consists of an organization of other's attitudes toward the person. In stage two, an organization of the social attitudes of the generalized other is added. The generalized other is the organized community or social group which provides the individual with his unity of self. The attitude of the generalized other is the attitude of the whole community. To the extent that a person responds socially to an object (animate or inanimate), that object can become part of the generalized other. The community exerts control over the individual's behavior through the generalized other, for it is in this form that the social process or community enters into the individual's thinking as a determinant factor. Thinking can only take place when the individual internalizes the attitude of the generalized other toward himself. Mead conceives of thinking as an internal dialogue between the person and the generalized other.

For Mead, a self is possible only to a creature that can be object to itself, a characteristic possible only in society through the use of language. The process underlying production of the self is role-taking, which occurs whenever significant symbols are used. One learns a significant symbol by sharing a sign that refers to a common course of experience with someone else. Every item of language carries with it some of the social matrix so that society penetrates an individual with each term he employs or acquires. There are many selves, and a multivariate personality is normal. An individual must become, due to interaction, a slightly different person to each new person with whom he interacts (Mead, 1934; Martindale, 1960).

As Mead and Cooley worked out the process of the formation of self through symbolic interaction with significant others in society, other psychologists and sociologists worked on reference group theory. Sherif proposed that self (he used the term ego) is primarily an internalization of the learned constellation of social norms acquired from one's social environment. Contact with these social norms builds attitudes which act as a frame of reference for behavior. Cantril (1965) suggested that self (he also used the term ego) could be determined by standards acquired from minority groups, discussion, or from the individual's own creative activity (Sargent and Williamson, 1966).

---

*Private conversation comparing notes on our manuscripts.

According to H. S. Sullivan (1965), the self-system is purely the product of interpersonal experience, arising from anxiety encountered in the pursuit of the satisfaction of general and zonal needs. Erikson conceived the basis for consciousness of identity as the two simultaneous observations: the immediate perception of one's self-sameness and continuity in time, and the simultaneous perception of the fact that others recognize one's sameness and continuity (DeLevita, 1965). P. A. Sorokin (1942) suggested that the behavior of an individual is largely determined by the groups of which he is a member, as is the content of his mentality. Through and from the group, the individual acquires, directly or indirectly, everything through interaction. Men possess both a biological and a social self. An individual has as many social selves as he is a member of social groups or social strata. The diversity of social role is the result of membership in a plurality of social groups.

Riesman (1950) suggested that one's personality reflects the form of society of which one is a member. In a "tradition-directed" society (*Gemeinschaft*-like) the young are inculcated with automatic obedience to tradition in roles defined from birth by the clan, age, and sex groups. In contrast, the individual growing up in an "inner-directed" society has implanted in him early in life the source of direction toward generalized but inescapably destined goals. He is generally socialized by his elders. The third typology is the "other-directed" society in which individuals are provided with their source of direction by their contemporaries. Contemporary American society is, in Riesman's view, an other-directed society.

Finally, the social encounter as a source of self has been developed by Goffman (1959, 1961b, 1963, 1967), his basic tenet being that societies everywhere must mobilize their members as self-regulating participants in social encounters. One method of mobilization for this purpose is through ritual: the individual is taught to have feelings attached to self and self expressed through face (in the oriental sense). There are some elements which must be built into a person if practical use is to be made of him for social interaction. The person becomes a construct, not of psychic properties, but from moral rules impressed upon him from without. It is the impression of these rules that causes an individual to become human.

In the *Presentation of Self in Everyday Life*, Goffman explains the generation of self through social interaction:

> In analyzing the self, then we are drawn from its possessor, from the person who will profit or lose most by it, for he and his body merely provide the peg on which something of a collaborative manufacture will be hung for a time. And the means for producing and maintaining selves do not reside inside the peg; in fact, these means are often bolted down in social establishments. There will be a back region with its tools

for shaping the body and a front region with its fixed props. There will be a team of persons whose activity on stage in conjunction with available props will constitute the scene from which the performed character's self will emerge, and another team, the audience, whose interpretive activity will be necessary for this emergence. The self is a product of all these arrangements, and in all of its parts bears the marks of this genesis. (Goffman, 1959, p. 253)*

In the review of this literature there is an agreement about (a) the existence of a social self and (b) the fact it derives from the social order rather than the reverse. The mechanics by which the social-self arises is not clear from the literature. Cooley, Mead, and Goffman, come very close to a complete understanding, but not quite.

I believe the processes involved in the generation of social self to include (1) recruitment, (2) socialization to a social role, inculcating the social identity associated with the role into the self-system, (3) legitimating such possession by means of a rite of passage (*see* Chapter 5 for a specific example), and (4) enactment of the patterns discussed in everyday life until (5) formal disengagement from that social role and identity. This schema subsumes two major ways of conceiving self and society to be twinborn: the introduction of society into self (1, 2, and 3 above) and the presentation of self (given legitimate face rights on the part of the individual) in some social occasion (4 above).

THE PSYCHOLOGICAL PERSPECTIVE

There is an endemic assumption among psychologists that self is more than a physiological flowering or entelechy unfolding. For many psychologists, Sherif's (1969) statement is taken as valid:

> The subsystem designed as self is a developmental formation. It is not present at birth. Once formed it is not immutable throughout life. Self develops as one's body and its parts are differentiated from the environment and as attitudes are formed defining modes of relatedness to various objects (including one's own body), persons, groups, and values in the socio-cultural setting. Throughout life, as the individual acquires new social ties, new roles, and changed status because of his accomplishments or his age, the self-system does change and must change if he is to behave consistently in terms of his altered relationships and responsibilities. (p. 386)

Sherif also notes that self (or ego) is a subsystem in the psychological makeup, as the Gestalt psychologists Koffka (1935), Kohler (1929), and Lewin (1935) emphasized.

(*Reprinted with permission of Doubleday & Company Inc, New York, from "The Presentation of Self in Everyday Life" by Erving Goffman. Copyright © 1959 by Doubleday & Company Inc.)

Sigmund Freud defines self as a system composed of the id (instincts), the superego (internalized social norms), and the ego (experiences of the mind, which is differentiated to act as a mediator for id, superego, and external reality) (Goldenweiser, 1940). The later and more pessimistic Freud stressed instincts of Thanatos (death) and Eros (life) as dominant over ego and superego in his model of man in the IIIC* exchange of letters with Einstein appeared to yield primacy to Thanatos. If nothing else, Freud served to legitimate among several generations of psychologists the view that society (superego) shared a portion of self, and that was enough among the infighting of behavioral scientists to resolve the question as to whether society was phenomena or epiphenomena. Freud's contribution here is as much political as scientific, perhaps more so.

For Jung, the self is the equivalent of the "psyche" or the total personality. It is the midpoint of the personality around which all other systems are constellated. Adler said that the self is a highly personalized, subjective system which interprets and makes meaningful the experiences of the organism. It searches for experience which will aid in the fulfilling of the person's unique style of life; and if such experiences are not available, the self attempts to create them (Hall and Lindsey, 1957). The self, as Harry Stack Sullivan (Ullman, 1965) defines it, is the various protective measures and supervisory controls which act to decrease the anxiety of interpersonal relationships by sanctioning or forbidding behavior.

For Symonds, the self is ways in which an individual reacts to himself. It consists of four aspects: (1) how a person perceives himself, (2) what he thinks of himself, (3) how he values himself, and (4) how he attempts through various actions to enhance or defend himself (Hall and Lindsey, 1957).

Very similar to Mead is Diggory's (1966) definition of self as a *relation* in which an agent and the object of his act are the same organism. I believe this is true enough, but only part of the necessary content of the concept. Snygg and Combs (1949) define a phenomenal self. It is an extremely stable organization, differentiated out of the phenomenal field (the totality of experience of which an individual is aware at the moment of action) and includes all those parts of the phenomenal field which the individual experiences as part or characteristic of himself. It is the only frame of reference which an individual possesses and as such gives continuity and consistency to his behavior.

In Sarbin's view, the self is a cognitive structure which consists of one's ideas about various aspects of one's being. It is composed of substructure

---

*International Institute of Intellectual Cooperation of the League of Nations. Cited in Sherif (1969), p. 225.

containing concepts of the body (the somatic self), of the sense organs and musculature (the receptor-effector self), and the social self. Hilgard says simply that the self is one's image of himself. Carl Rogers feels the self to be a differentiated portion of the phenomenal field consisting of conscious perceptions and values of the "I" or "me." Gardner Murphy says that the self is a person's perceptions and conceptions of his whole being, the individual as known to the individual (all in Hall and Lindsey, 1957).

Ruth Wylie (1961), in her review of the psychological literature on the self, finds that the term is used in two separate ways. There is the self as subject or agent and the self as object, as the individual known to himself. She defines the phenomenal self as the conscious self-concept which determines the person's behavior.

William James considers the social self to be an outgrowth of the interplay of instincts and habits in a predominantly social environment. He describes a self as being composed of the "I," self as known, one of the things in its conscious. The empirical self, the "me," is the sum total of what a person can call his. Such a self typically arouses feelings and emotions of self-appreciation, and prompts action of self-seeking actions and self-preservation. Its constituents include: the material me, encompassing all the body and successive circles of friends associated with it (one's clothes, family, home, up to and all possessions); the social me which is the recognition one gets from others (one may have as many social selves as there are individuals who recognize him); and the spiritual me, a collection of one's states of consciousness and psychic facilities (Martindale, 1960; also Young and Oberdorfer, 1940).

Even a cursory examination of the field of psychology leaves little doubt that in the field there is a strong assumption that society gives shape to self. And the Group for the Advancement of Psychiatry (1964) rejected instinct as the source of aggressive human behavior in its statement that "war is a social institution; it is not inevitably rooted in the nature of man" (cited in Sherif, 1969).

An Operational Definition of Self-system

According to Mead (1934), the self is composed of various "elementary selves" which answers to the various aspects of the structure of the social process. The structure of the complete self is thus a reflection of the entire social process. I believe that Mead in this analysis, provides us with a methodology for the determination of the way self fits social order. The key to this methodology is the notion of "social identity." We will postulate that the elementary self which reflects a given social process is the epistemic correlate of the concept *social identity*.

Thus, for the social process of family life, one such elementary self is referred to as "daughter." "I am a daughter," says she who is involved in the family process. Blumer says, somewhere, that the notion of the mother without the child is a nonsense notion. We refer to the female who takes up the activities reserved for a young girl in the household. Unmarried, residing with her parents as the "daughter," she thinks of herself as a "daughter," and organizes her behavior accordingly.

There are any number of social identities; they answer to many, many of the lines of action (processes) in a society. These social identities are postulated to constitute the major link between self and society. We need to know how many of these links (social identities) there are in the self-system of a given individual and what ratio of social identities occurs in conjunction with other behavior-organizing components of the self-system (e.g., I am hot-tempered). If we know the above, we can begin to know the degree to which self and society are linked.

Twenty Statements Test

If we want to know what the key components of the self-system are, the direct approach is to ask people to tell us. The Twenty Statements Test (TST) of Manford Kuhn (1954) and his students can be adapted to serve the purpose. Kuhn asked people to respond to a simple question "Who Am I?" 20 times. From the data, the authors discovered a set of "consensual" items that reflected social structural anchorages. If we make the assumption that a given person makes a quick inventory of the components of his self-system when responding to such a question and, assume farther, that such an inventory yields a fairly exhaustive and valid listing of the chief components of the self-structure, then we can code those components into two major categories: social takes and psyche takes.

Of course there are any number of reasons why a self-reported inventory of self-system components might be a problem to use as the basis for an operational definition of "self." The person might respond differently from time 1 to time 2. The self-system may contain components inaccessible to the individual. The social desirability of some responses serves to foreclose reporting. But, by and large, I think that the experience that Kuhn has had (and the hundreds I have administered) show that the self-system is quite well revealed by the TST. In any event, *social selves* should be accessible to most persons (short of sheer stupidity or deliberate deception) if, as Mead says, one continually receives information from others about his social self.

Given a coding procedure for separating social takes from more personal components of the self-system, it becomes a matter of simple calculation to determine what percentage of the items reported have corresponded to the social structure and which are nonsocial adopted and internalized components. The ratio of social takes to psychological takes then provides an operational and empirically derived measurement of the degree to which self and society are twinborn.

Operational Definitions of Social Takes

In this section I want to report the procedures I am using to distinguish between (1) psychological takes and (2) social takes in addition to (2a) life-long social takes, (2b) long social takes, and (2c) short takes. The operations given here are far from complete. The reasons for presenting them at this time are manifold. I want to clarify the ways one understands the self-society link; I want to emphasize that self may not be coterminous with society; and I would like to stimulate a dialectic on the question of the sources of self, besides quantifying the relative input of each source.

Psyche Takes and Social Takes

I operationally code an item reported in the TST which has no social organizational base as a psychological take. This means that there is no group *qua* group which generates behavior; for example, if one states, in response to the question: "Who am I?" that "I am a searcher," then this is coded as a psyche take. There is no social system with that characteristic in that meaning as a component of the role expectations nor any such *named* social identity.

However, if one says that "I am a student," it is coded as a social take; there is an associated social role; the behavior organized by that take is fairly specific and publicly known. There are external controls to keep people uptight to the social take and there are rewards, culturally established, allocated to adequate performance of the activity. All those facts help one determine the coding of specific items as socially based self-components. In addition, for social takes, it is accepted that some agent of society has the right to probe one's psyche in order to judge the degree of fit between self and society. This probing is variously expressed in tests, oaths, and disquisitions. If there is a mismatch between self and social order, then re-training, resocialization, rehabilitation, reforming, and "psychiatry" are standard processes in the social order to which people are subjected. For privately organized components of the self-systems, these processes are not brought to bear. In either case, probing the psyche and "repairing" it, one has a clue that the self-component in question keys off the social system; if no such process is seen to be relevant to the TST item, then one can code it a nonsocial or "psyche take."

Aside from the foregoing, there are other clues which aid in coding between social and more purely private components of the self-system. Among these are included *checking*: if there are *checking* routines before expressing the behavior in question, then it probably is a social take.* For example, if one checks (or is checked out by others) before enacting that behavior character- istic of a "soldier" or "policeman" as in the instance of their standing inspec- tion before going on duty, or in the case of a housewife checking out at the supermarket, or a student checking out of the dorm, then there is probably a social identity underwriting the behavior in question and the item should be coded "social take."

There are many problems inherent in searching out the social basis of the self-system. One such problem is how to code responses such as: I am ambi- tious; I am diligent; I am loyal; I am romantic; I am friendly; I am cautious; I am frugal; I am trusting; I am aggressive, and so on. All of these, if reported self-system components, clearly are related to the social order. But as they do not have a specific social identity as an anchorage point in the social system, I code them psyche takes. There are no rites-of-passage, no celebra- tion in public (as at confirmation) that one is now one of these things, and there is little effort to hold one publicly accountable for the performance related to the item.

The items immediately above are, however, deeply rooted in the culture and aid enormously in carrying out one's social roles, but the fact that they were adduced rather than specific social identities in response to the question "Who am I?" means, I assume, that such social identities are unclaimable and more importantly, that self is not yet lodged in social order.

There are a great many items reported in TST inventories of self which have even less connection to the social order. These too are coded psyche takes: I am curious; I am moody; I am self-conscious; I am temperamental; I am contemplative; I am fat; I am beautiful; I am tired; I am young; I am easily hurt, and so on. There is very little social structural support in our society for "being" fat, and less to be found in the cultural order. While some people belong to TOPS, a fat people's organization, the chances are that the behavior organized in "being" fat bears more to the organization of the psychology of it all than the sociology.

In some societies, age grades are closely shaped by the culture and one finds a clear differentiation in that society for age-organized behavior. Eisenstadt

---

*I am indebted to Sam Burns for this idea.

(1956) has provided us with an excellent survey of age groups among the Nuer, the Nandi, the Plains Indians, the Yako, the Swazi, the Nupe, and the Nyakyusa, among others. For these societies, the response, "I am *young*," is a social take. In those societies where these social identities and their social structural supports have been obliterated by industrialization, such responses take on the characteristics of a psyche take. For our society, there are still some social structural supports for this self-structure, but no great support is provided to us in the social order—no rites of passage, no assumption of specific duties, no checking, few social controls, and so on. As I have said, to code it is a problem; but, on balance, I think it is more a privately held component than specifically linked to the social order. In support of this one must consider the fact that many "old" people do "young" things and many young people do "older" things. Since few complex organizations support them, age-grades become obliterated as a feature of the social order. The behavior associated with age-grades becomes available for private uses.

Long Takes and Short Takes

If one is able to separate social takes from psyche takes, the next question is how to distinguish between short takes and long takes. The basic guide I use here is the time dimension. If one is involved in the role for but a brief time—four years or four months or four hours—then it is coded as a short take. In conjunction with time, if one can enter and leave the social role with little fuss or bother, a simple farewell or less, it is operationally construed to be a short take. If the role take requires a rite of passage or other public ceremony before enactment then it probably is a long or lifelong take. If one really believes he is such a thing, it probably is a long take. For example, I have a friend who thinks he is an M.D. When I telephone him, he says, "Hello, this is Dr. Smith." When I reply, I say, "Hello, Ed. this is Dick Young." He is a doctor and views himself to be one at home and at office. I believe myself to be a sociologist but not to the same extent that Ed Smith believes himself to be a "doctor."

A third important aspect of a short take is the range of behavior it encompasses. Short takes evoke as few as one or two specific unit acts—purchase of a ticket and attendance, a signature and periodic check writing, a nod and a brief conversation. Sometimes the short take involves a complex series of unit acts as in the example of a "patient" or a "guest." Sometimes short takes involve a contract in which specific but restricted acts are called forth. In all events, the range of behavior involved is much smaller than that of a long take.

Now as to the task: if self arises from society, what happens when self and society are separated? There are two answers: a tragic one and a more optimistic one. In Chapter 4, I shall review the tragic version in a discussion of Marcuse, Marx, and others. The more optimistic view is discussed in two parts. In Chapter 5, I shall review the position that the separation of self from large-scale organization is an eminently "rational" process. If one is to eliminate the less predictable from shaping the destiny of the organization *qua* organization, then one must replace self-system as a major structural support for that organization with a cybernation technology.

It is in the final two chapters where one will find a carefully qualified statement about the possibilities inherent in the advent of large-scale organizations for the self-system. If we assume that the self can arise from sources other than large-scale organizations or in patterns strikingly different from the table of organization of mass society, then the separation of self from society is as much a promise as it is tragedy. In these two chapters I present several arenas wherein self can be obtained. Most of these resources for self are taking preliminary form and doubtlessly will change form . . . but at present, these should not be a cause for panic nor for repression. They should be understood for what they are—a rich source of self to replace the social identities lost to us with the evolution of *Gemeinschaft* to postindustrial *Gesellschaft*. As churches, schools, industry, business, and recreation apply the technology of the technetronic society to their organizational problems, individuals must turn to new sources of self if we are to remain human. The separation of self from mass society need not be tragic if we are successful in understanding our destiny.

CHAPTER 4

Self and Society Separated: The Tragic Version

THE TRAGIC VERSION

Given that there is no alternative source of self-structure and given that social systems cannot survive without using a social identity as the primary structural support, then separation of the two is tragic. In such a society there is alienation and the ". . . alienated man is everyman and no man, drifting in a world that has little meaning for him and over which he exercises little power, a stranger to himself and others" (Josephsons, 1964, p. 11).

ALIENATED LABOR

From the point of view of the social psychologist, the writings of Marx are indispensible; they mark the beginning of our understanding of the social sources of happiness and of despair, of violence and of love, of worship and of war. Whatever else they are, these writings focus the theorist's attention upon the social sources of behavior, feeling, and thought. After reading Marx one cannot turn to instincts, urges, attitudes, entelechies, spirits, and Gods in order to understand the meaning and tragedy of life . . . with Marx, we have lost most of our innocence . . . now we become responsible.

In the passages below, we note that the center of attention is the "worker." There are two points to focus upon: (a) that the term, "worker" is a social identity keying off from the division of labor in the social order, and (b) that this identity is assumed to represent a necessary structure of the self-system. It is the last point which we must reexamine in Chapter 5.

In his essay Alienated Labor (1844), Marx perceived only too well that the

27

0342207

018257

fate of man was linked to the fate of society; as society was a class system, it separates him from his creative social identity, that of "worker":

> What then do we mean by the alienation of labor? First, that the work he performs is extraneous to the worker, that is, it is not personal to him, is not part of his nature; therefore he does not fulfill himself in work, but actually denies himself; feels miserable rather than content, cannot freely develop his physical and mental powers, but instead becomes physically exhausted and mentally debased. Only while not working can the worker be himself; for while at work he experiences himself as a stranger. Therefore only during leisure hours does he feel at home, while at work he feels homeless. His labor is not voluntary, but coerced, forced labor. It satisfies no spontaneous creative urge, but is only a means for the satisfaction of wants which have nothing to do with work. Its alien character therefore is revealed by the fact that, when no physical or other compulsion exists, work is avoided like the plague. (Josephsons, 1962, p. 97)*

Under the condition of social organization wherein one's self-system arises from the social system, then the tragedy which besets the worker *qua* social identity besets the individual *qua* human. In such a case one is doubly hurt— once in shattering his most cherished and most meaningful self-source, and then as the product of his labor is turned back upon him as a weapon to enslave him in this tragic condition:

> From this premise it is clear that the more the worker exerts himself, the more powerful becomes the world of things which he creates and which confront him as alien objects; hence the poorer he becomes in his inner life, and the less belongs to him as his own. It is the same with religion. The more man puts into God, the less he retains in himself. The worker puts his life into the things he makes; and his life then belongs to him no more, but to the product of his labor. The greater the worker's activity, therefore, the more pointless his life becomes. (Josephsons, 1962, p. 95)

The dehumanizing process reduces man to a mere animal, and therein lies the wellspring of the Marxian rage toward such a social order, and therein lies, as well, the appeal of Marx to the humanist:

> As a result, man—the worker—feels freely active only in his animal functions—dating, drinking, procreating, or at most in his dwelling and personal adornment—while in his human and social functions he is reduced to an animal. The animal becomes human, and the human becomes animal. Certainly eating, drinking, and proceating are also genuinely human functions; but abstractly considered, apart from all other human activities and regarded as ultimate ends in themselves, they are merely animal functions. (Josephsons, 1962, p. 98)

But man is more than "the worker" and, as computer science is organized as a cybernetic control system, then man is liberated from a social identity which must, under conditions of mass and precise production, be alienating.

(*From "Alienated Labor" by Karl Marx, translated by Eric and Mary Josephson. From the book "Man Alone" edited by Eric and Mary Josephson. Copyright © 1962 by Dell Publishing Co., Inc. Reprinted by permission of the publisher.)

But what will serve as new sources of self if self is essential to the human condition? More of this in Chapter 6.

*The Moral Order**

As much as he wanted a sociology, Durkheim wanted a moral order to stabilize and to comfort man rather than to estrange him and lead him to suicide. Thus the interest of Durkheim in solidarity. Its forms and its destruction were as much of interest to Durkheim in their consequences at the personal level as was his interest in an accurate analysis of society. Durkheim suffered under a dual discontinuity between self-system and the social order; above all he was a "Jew" and a "Frenchman" in some of the most turbulent times in the history of France. Both social identities keyed off the organization of social systems and both created considerable anguish for him.

For one born in a society where self and social order were twinborn, the solution to any discomfort at the personal level must be found in the moral (normative) order, even if it leads to authoritarianism with a trade-off of freedom for more "order" in the social order. In a society where self might arise from nonsocial sources, the problems in the normative structure of LSO could have less meaning for personal troubles than in Durkheim's time.

In reading Durkheim's statement that for every individual fact there is a social fact, one's attention is drawn to the tragic consequences of an anomic era. If man's consciousness and character were inevitably tied to LSOs, then something akin to the Luddite solution or the fascist solution might be required. But if self has a source other than the role differentiations of society, then an unstable social order has less than direct and immediate pain for the person—a possibility which needs to be well-considered before binding self to society too tightly. It is a basic assumption of modern systems theory that social systems must remain mapped to their environment if they are going to be able to transfer the order in the environment to order in the system. Under conditions of a stable environment, a stable mapping of the moral order is appropriate. When the self-system depends upon the moral order, then an unstable or ultrastable moral order creates personal problems. Under conditions of a changing environment, a stable moral order is impossible; and so tying self to such a moral order is impossible. The moral order also becomes a poor source of self under the condition that the social system must seek and adopt variety in order to remain in match to its environment.

---

*One must keep in mind the fact that for Durkheim, "moral order" means the rules of the game more than it means following God. If this point is lost, the discussion which follows is lost.

A case in point is the foreign policy of the United States. If the political system of the United States is to remain mapped to a changing environment, then it may have to change its policy (moral order) in respect to Communist nations. For one to view one's own self as "anti-communist" means to run the risk of having one's self-structure damaged when the foreign policy of the United States is changed, as change it will.

The Organization Man

The soul of man is tossed and teased with the vicissitudes of society in the Durkheimian analysis. It is torn and trapped in the Marxian analysis. In the analysis of William H. Whyte, Jr. (1956) there is another tragic consequence: the self-system of man is tailored and trimmed to suit the large-scale organization. The corporation, government bureaus, universities, labor unions, the military—in each one gives up hope, ambition, and individuality in exchange for status, security, and not least, affluence.

For the organization man, the social identity in the table of organization preempts his self-system for that period of time during which he occupies it. But it is not anchored too firmly to the self-system, since the name of the game is to move into another niche. In *this* tragedy, a succession of social identities replace each other; mobility brings the intimation of separation between self and society. But only an intimation; while the organization man is in the role, he maps his behavior to it with fervor, with skill, with dedication, and with care. His home is a branch office; his wife, a lieutenant. For the organization man, his friends are selected by the requirements of office, and his church selected by its usefulness to his job.

The social ethic which underwrites the behavior of the organization man requires that he sacrifice his beliefs, the richness of his traditional religion, his family, and his self in order to remain in the system. Whyte is not alone in his concern with the quiet, smooth, comfortable linkage between self and large-scale organization. Baker (1969) has done an analysis of postwar popular fiction in terms of what such a source of identity does to man from the novelist's point of view.

> The insignificance and alienation of the individual in society is fully documented by the postwar novelists. It first emerges in the postwar novels of Mailer and Shaw, where the individual suddenly confronts his insignificance and impotence in the monolithic structure of the military organization. Industrialism, furthermore, is represented as the cause that makes man lose his significance and meaning. It leads, as Taylor Caldwell at one point suggests, to the destruction of "man's sense of his innate integrity."
>
> The meaninglessness of the individual and life—alienation—is graphically depicted in the restlessness and unhappiness of Marquand's Charles Gray (in *Point of No Return*)

and Wilson's Tom Rath (in *The Man in the Gray Flannel Suit*). "But do we *know* each other? Does anybody around here really know anybody else?" questions a disillusioned acquaintance of Gray's. And Sidney Skelton, in *Melville Goodwin, USA*, looking retrospectively at his own life, recalls with sadness that man's life is often shaped by external forces over which he has little or no control, until at last he becomes "something that he never exactly wanted to be." This meaninglessness is seen in Tom Rath's wife. "We shouldn't be so discontented all the time," she states, but she cannot comprehend the cause for it. And, as General Cummings notes elsewhere, "The natural role of twentieth-century man is anxiety."

Convergent with this viewpoint of the relative insignificance of the individual and the disillusionment and futility of existence is the belief that the future holds little of worth. The American Dream is viewed with skepticism if not disbelief. What happened to the Dream—of equal opportunity, individualism, freedom, diversity? Betty Smith's bestseller of the war years, *A Tree Grows in Brooklyn* (1943) sounds a hopeful note; but even the title of her 1948 bestseller is prophetic: *Tomorrow Will Be Better*. But will it? Henny, Margie Shannon's father in the latter book, wonders.

. . . The Great American Dream had betrayed Henny. But why couldn't it work for Frankie. . . .

Yes, the Great American Dream had betrayed Henny. Sometimes he wondered whether it had ever existed in the first place.

This disillusionment is quite prominent in the novels of O'Hara. Grace Caldwell (*A Rage to Live*, 1949) leads a spiritually impoverished life in which promiscuous affairs serve as brief interludes in her flight from reality; Joe Chapin (*Ten North Frederick*, 1955), a man of principles and ideals, is broken and disillusioned by his experience in politics; and Raymond Eaton (*From the Terrace*, 1958), an energetic industrialist, finds himself, at middle age, adrift in a meaningless universe. Taylor Caldwell, too, reflects this disillusionment. Hopeful of America's future shortly after World War II (*This Side of Innocence*, 1946), her faith in man and America waned in future years (*Never Victorious, Never Defeated*, 1954), until, finally, she turned to studies of religion (*Dear and Glorious Physician*, 1959). (cited in Baker and Sheldon, p. 19–20.)*

MARCUSE

In the Marcusean analysis, mechanization saves not only time, energy, and expense but saves "libido" as well (1964). The energy of the life instincts expressed in handicraft, sailing, baking, and other pretechnical occupations has been "saved" in the post-technical modes of production: assembly line, automation, and modern conveniences. But "saved" is a smooth and subtle way to refer to what has happened which prevents the theorist from understanding what post-industrial society has done to people. It has reduced man's

(*Reprinted with permission of Glencoe Press (*Beverly Hills, California*) a Division of The Macmillan Company from "*Post War America: The Search for Identity*" by Donald G. Baker & Charles H. Shelden. Copyright © 1969 by Glencoe Press, a Division of the Macmillan Company.)

capacity to express his life instincts in socially constructive, albeit primitive, modes. Post-industrial society does not require the Freudian core of the self: the very life instincts themselves. Therein lies the tragedy, played on a grand scale and presided over by the most competent of those in management, accounting, data processing, finance, marketing, office administration, personnel, production, and vocational training—experts turned out smoothly and rationally by the modern public university. In the Marcusean analysis, technology limits the scope of self and reduces the need for self.

However much one agrees with this analysis, expanded to the length and breadth of experience, it does not follow that the way to restore dignity, dimension, and energy to self is by either one of the double options of the "great refusal" or by shattering social organization.

A third option exists and receives hesitant support from Marcuse. After rejecting a recent Norman Brown advocacy of an highly personalized and privatized erotic consciousness, Marcuse suggests that an authentic society requires a public and political relationship between the liberated person and the whole community:

> ". . . The eroticized body would rebel against exploitation, competition, false virility, conquest of space, and violation of nature—all the established conditions. In this context we can say that the seeds of revolution lie in the emancipation of the senses (Marx)—but only when the senses become practical, productive forces in changing reality." (*Psychology Today.* Feb. 1971; p. 64).

This position is curiously similar to that of Charles Reich (1970), to whom the revolution depends upon change from within the institutions of the corporate state. These institutions, while highly resistive to change from without, are highly vulnerable to change from within. In as much as the power of the corporate state depended upon "Consciousness II," that power diminishes as "Consciousness III" develops among the employees. In the Reichian analysis, Consciousness III infiltrates the establishment and eventually transforms the corporation to human ends. My own view is that the corporation becomes less dependent upon psychological states as technology of data control improves. The authentic society demands both new sources of self at the psychological level and political control of the corporation at the sociological level. Each is a separate enterprize and both crucial to the emergence of an authentic society.

I expect both sociology and psychology to be foster parents to the development of new sources of self in the very near future. Although this seems unlikely in 1970, already there is a sociology liberation movement (SLM) to unchain sociology from serving establishment and, in psychology, on the west coast there is a huge psychology underground. I expect both the SLM and the psychology underground to change the orientations of each discipline. In the case of psychology, it will cease betraying the Freudian vision, thanks chiefly to Marcuse's impact. Modern revisionists in sociology will cease betraying the visions of Marx and Lester Ward, thanks to the efforts of Richard Flacks, Martin Nicolaus, Bob Ross, and John Leggett, among others in the SLM.

I expect that technology will be put to use to supply elements of self but the monopology of establishment society over the production and shaping of self in its own image is rapidly disappearing. This does not mean that the more global criticisms of Marcuse about post-industrial society are to be set aside lightly. The evils of a market system in aimless pursuit of growth, outside the control of the political system if not in league with it, is one of the major problems prior to *any* kind of use or source of self. Things are going wrong in the world in a monumental way—starvation of self and of body, senseless wars in Southeast Asia, pollution of the earth, waste of resource, violence in the cities, homelessness of millions; all are testimony to the foolishness of a state capitalism moving to the world stage led by U.S. "foreign" policy. Without dealing with Marcuse on other questions, it would be idle to dismiss Marcuse on the tragic relation between self and post-industrial society exemplified by the United States.*

SOCIOTECHNICS

Stanley Hetzler (1967), in generating a new set of hypotheses for development, discusses at length the interface between self-system and technology in his section on the man-machine organization. The general point is that power systems are constituted in such a way in the earlier stages of technological evolution that there is a link between tools and notions of what it is that a man is. The story is that in a society where self is part of the technology then self becomes an obstacle to development. Societies having a preponderance of longtake social identities must first obliterate those self-systems if they are going to "progress." Such societies require as much supervision and coercion to introduce a new tool, machine, or technique as to induce German, Italian, Polish, or Navajo people to conceive of themselves as "Americans."

Societies with short takes as the typical unit of role involvement in LSOs have a technical advantage over folk societies in that the social take involved

---

*I must apologize for this cavalier treatment of Marcuse. Given the present conditions, his analysis is much more trenchant and pressing than is mine. My analysis may be the more valid only if the forces of repression and manipulation can be constrained so that new sources of self are permitted to develop.

does not become interfaced with the self-system of the technician, and it is a rather simpler matter to replace technical roles in "advanced societies". In the pursuit of development, it is rational to obliterate social identities as the economy moves from technology to technology. It is even more rational to sever the social psychological tie between technology and technician in the course of adopting new tools and techniques.

The question arises whether it is better to retain a technology which is eminently rational but whose social psychological consequences are tragic beyond measure. In such a society one beholds the works that his hands have wrought and the labor that he has labored to do and comes to understand that all is vanity and vexation of the spirit—that there is indeed no profit under the sun. But this dichotomy of choice between self and "modern" technology is a false dichotomy. There is another choice. It is possible to conceive of a social organization where large-scale establishments are separated from the generation of self and are freed (and controlled) to do what they best can do: produce essential social services and commodities and distribute these to a mass society. Health, food, shelter, banking, science, knowledge, trade, transportation are essential and should be rationalized. The problems of pollution, population control, racism, exploitation, and militarism require the services of large-scale establishments rationally organized in order to obtain movement on these problems. This third choice includes the necessity that, in a different arena, the generation of self goes on in directions unlimited by the constraints of a narrow "rationality."

THE GENERATION OF SELF IN MODERN SOCIETY

A catalog of those who hold that the marriage between self and society is sick runs into the thousands; most of these analysts assume the solution lies in something akin to marriage counseling: straighten out the structure of self (social work) or of society (social revolution) in order to reduce the mismatch between self and society. There is a third alternative which the young appear to be taking in their naïve, nonpolitical, enthusiastic way: to drop out from establishment society and seek new sources of self. Why should one choose to suffer the fate of one's parents if all of the novelists, sociologists, and polemicists are correct? In order to save Bell Telephone, I.T.&T., the Agriculture Department, Colorado State University, the Marine Corps, General Mills, Prudential Life Insurance, or Gulf Oil Company? Such organizations are stable beyond the aid or animosity of a young person; they do not need *him*, only some small part of his money; he has no self at stake in their fate, only a minor inconvenience while the corporation closes or opens another branch, dumps more pollution, uses more of nature's bounty, or pays two cents less in dividends to his dad.

When one examines the institutions of urban life in terms of the efficacy of each in generating and supporting an estimable and satisfying self-system, one turns away in despair. From a technical point of view, the nuclear family is a poor place for self to develop. In folk societies, the "mother" was surrounded by more mature and more experienced women to aid her in the rearing of "her" children. There were clear-cut social identities as well as established phases of child development which gave guidance to the mother. In complex societies, the nuclear family is isolated from the larger kin group except for short visits. The socialization function is beyond its capacity. The young mother has little sense of direction to go in the socialization process with her children. All this means that she is poorly equipped in terms of resources to effect the socialization alone. She is reduced to piecemeal *post hoc* response couched in negative terms about what her children should not do. This is in contrast to the rich and regulated resources at the disposal of mothers in other cultures. For the urban family as well, the father is lost to the socialization process. More importantly, his models for self are lost to his sons.

The churches do not provide a *continuing* milieu in which the self is the central focus of attention. The church does have a rich potential for the construction of the self-system of youngsters in the city, but many pastors prefer to turn their attention to mortgages and missions, to pressing social issues, to questions of salvation, or to the abstract questions left over from divinity school. What small attention to self given by the ecclesiasts is, again, piecemeal and of short duration, far too short for an adequate job to be done. In the church itself, a sermon may be relevant in general terms to the human condition, or a given program may be offered every Thursday evening in family life, but the hard, sustained interest in self-system found, for example, in the traditional Catholic Church is missing in the urban centers.

In the city, the major institution charged with socialization is the school system yet the educational system is organized to teach subjects rather than people. There is much payoff for socialization in the curricula of the schools, to be sure. But that socialization does not lead to a coherent and unitary self-system. The two worlds of childhood outlined by Bronfenbrenner (1969) provide an invidious contrast between the childhood experience of the Soviet child and the American child. For the Soviet child, the educational experience is a sustained exercise in self-discipline organized by the key values out of which any social system may be constructed: joint activity, honesty, friendliness, self-reliance, and cooperation. Moral training and character building are as important as maths, reading, and communist theory in the early years.

On the other hand, the U.S. child is exposed to an experience in which there is considerable ambivalence about moral training. The historical fact is that morality as such is intimately (and unnecessarily) tied to religion, and the first amendment forbids establishing religion by governmental units. Until Kalamazoo in 1872, most schools were private and could teach religion (and thereby morality) without conflict with the Constitution. The school system cops out in America by teaching subject matter rather than children. Couple that fact with the uniform mediocracy of faculty and students in educational departments from Michigan to Columbia to Mississippi and one begins to understand the terrible destiny of our children.

The family is not geared to socialize the child; most mothers are not adequate to the task because they work or lack the tools. The Church is a painful hour for older children and a fun hour for small children once a week. Bible school is more organized for the merchandise of tribal myths than for contemporary selfhood.

TV, before which much of life is learned, is a poor medium for morality. Murder, violence, and bizarre family situations are the stock-in-trade of TV. The obscene use of sex to sell cigarettes and soap, the evil advantage taken to exploit parent-child hostility, the more insidious programming of the child as a portable commercial machine cannot begin to be useful in the building of a self-system that is satisfying and adequate to the task of human existence.

Peer groups have taken over the larger burden of socialization, again without the tools with which to work for most age grades. Psychological drives, wants, wishes, proclivities, urges, interests, and needs do not become mediated by a self-system in that the children themselves are the rankest amateurs in self-development, self-control, self-respect, self-discipline, self-fulfillment, and self-actualization.

The fate of our children is a political question. Power must be wrested from the school administrators, from the teacher unions, and the NEA by an organized corps of young teachers and students. Power must be wrested from the faculty and administration by young professors and education majors. Power must be wrested from the school boards by the PTA, or school boards will continue to use the school curricula for business, commerce, and industrial purposes rather than human fulfillment.

Bronfenbrenner has provided the rationale for this political act. As yet no one has reached the masses with a message clear enough to spell out the immediacy of the danger. Organized parents, students, and teachers must turn to the task.

If the church, school, and family are not geared to produce an effective self, there seems little point in surveying the other institutions of the city for their possibilities in socialization. Theatres, restaurants, clothing stores, parking lots, police, ice cream kiosks, bars, hamburger drive-ins, vacant lots, and pawn shops all have some importance to the generation of self for some people—but most have little or no meaning for *most* people in this respect. In small-town America, the ice cream parlor provided a place to *be* (or learn to be) a particular kind of social self. Taverns and bars are supportive to certain social identities, e.g., males and Germans for example. Whatever the potential of these places as structural supports for cherished social identities, the fact is that from the point of view of management they are a secondary interest in mass society. Even if they were a primary interest from the point of view of the customer, and I think that is sometimes the case, such places, as they function in contemporary cities, are too meagre and too restricted in possibilities to do a first-rate job. Thinking about the places in the modern city where an adequate self-structure might develop, one remains puzzled. Whatever else it does, the city is simply not geared to that particular task. The result is that the most effective socialization to the most inadequate models occurs in the peer group: gangs, cliques, friends, and, most ominously, the military.

The modern city has destroyed the rich street life in which identity was patterned and stabilized in the company of adults, and which was found in the pre-industrial city. What street life is left has no pattern for self and less support from interested adults. By destroying street life, by isolating the mother, by removing the father from his sons, by turning religion and schools to other uses, by rationalizing occupations, we have effectively destroyed the sources of self in the city. As a result, we threaten to produce a generation of savages—with little or no self-structure, little or no feedback, little or no self-experience. A generation of people socialized to a teenage culture or to less organizing components of the self is not a generation to be trusted to decide the fate of the world, or even their own fate inasmuch as that fate unavoidably touches others. New sources of self are required in cities, new media in which the self is the central interest. In addition, new uses of self must be found if society is to survive its rationality. If they are not, the tragic version takes precedence over the rational version, and we are left with beautifully constructed large-scale organizations and shoddily constructed self-systems.

CHAPTER 5

Society Without Self:
The Rational Version

THE RATIONAL VERSION

As stated earlier, the central interest of this monograph is to explore the conditions of social organization under which self and society are or are not twinborn. In that interest we shall examine the processes by which self is linked to social structure and inquire whether these processes are operative in the large-scale organizations typically found in a complex industrial society.

SHORT TAKES AND SELF-SYSTEMS

In folk societies, social structure is generated by means of long and lifelong social identities plugged into the self-system by means of socialization and by rites of passage. A person typically goes through a socialization process by which social identities are mapped out in a configurational way and then transferred to the self-structure. These social identities then constitute "that which one is" and organize behavior in ways compatible with specific social maps. Thus, one was socialized to be a Catholic and/or a man and/or a German and, in specific definitions of the situation, one refers to the relevant social identity in his self-inventory, uses it as the reference point, matches his behavior to that reference point in consonance with others, and in adjustment to exigencies arising in the occasion. When this occurs, order is transferred from physiological and psychological levels of existence to a social level of systems operation and organization. In this model, the self is a centrally important support for the social order. The set of social identities inculcated into the self-structure closely paralleled the social organization of a "simple society." Taken together, the social identities of all persons fit precisely the social organization of the folk society in question.

As large-scale organizations became the typical units of social experience and organization, different strategies of generating society were adopted.* The structure of LSO forbids self-involvement on the part of the masses processed through it. The system simply cannot make involvement in any given LSO contingent upon possession of the "right" social identity. LSOs cannot efficiently socialize and allocate social identities as the means to construct the system; it is irrational. However, some still do, as, for example, the army and the church. But most do not. G.M., King Soopers, Ward's, Ford, and a host of other LSOs cannot use social identities as a means to involve people.

LSOs require only that a small portion of a mass society map a small portion of their behavior to one or two normative expectations of that LSO once or twice a year. With such small input from such huge members, a LSO is able to transfer order from environment and to gain and elaborate structure as well, and thus is said to be more rationally organized.

But such small input does not require a corresponding structure in the self-system. For example, a bank can operate without any single customer going through a socialization process and without the social identity "customer" inculcated as an enduring component of the self-structure.

The social takes in a bank are short takes. As the bank becomes more "rationally" organized, less and less of the psychobiological capacities of humans is required to pull off the assembly of a social system. As the takes become shorter, self becomes less necessary. It is one of the ironies of rationality that society becomes independent of self as organizations become "better" managed. This does not mean that human behavior is not required in order to generate a social system; far from it—only that such behavior need not emerge out of one of the social identities constitutive of the self-system. This point is central to the question of the relationship between self-structure and social structure.

THE LOOKING-GLASS PROCESS

In folk societies, with face-to-face interaction as the medium of information flow, the looking-glass process is possible. In a mass society, with mass

---

*I refer to such a society as a "yellow-page society." A rough way of knowing when a society becomes independent of the self-system is by a determination that half or more of the pages in a telephone book are yellow.

communication as the media of information flow, the ongoing feedback required for the generation of self becomes less accurate, less continuous, and less focused upon the self-structure, or disappears entirely. A typical mass media is a lecture class of 200 in Economics 100. Given that media, there is little opportunity for the looking-glass process to operate; there is still less focus on the goodness of fit of self-structure as exists in contrast to self-structure as "should" exist. In my classes, for example, very seldom do I perceive people as discrete entities; still less do I comment upon their *self*. I do not tell students that they have a nice smile, a gentle way, an abrasive tone, or a weak moral structure, even had I some way to know such. Such feedback is defined as irrelevant to the given line of meaning. Apart from a little feedback upon narrow points of theory or fact, feedback in most college classes bears only small meaning even to the identity of student—itself a short take and hardly appropriate to the human condition. As Fromm would say, such a social take is far too one-sidedly cerebral. In most of the waking hours, for most of the people tied to large-scale establishments, the looking-glass process simply does not occur. Thus, a major assumption of the symbolic interactionists does not hold. As a symbolic interactionist, I understand that the looking-glass process is crucial to the experience and, thus, existence of self . . . but the looking glass is not there. At present, one must go through the looking glass to find self—and that can be a bad trip. In a graduate seminar, the looking-glass process is possible as there is a model of "professional" comportment presented and taken by the student as a holistic cognitive mapping. The graduate students involved are judged more on the degree to which they map their behavior to the role model than to the degree that any specific item of information is transmitted (although information flow is facilitated by internalizing the cognitive whole of "being" a sociologist, for example). It is something of a quandary that many of the officers, managers, and administrators who govern mass society have had the benefit of a rich and challenging socialization experience in professional schools, such as the law, medicine, science, business, and so on, yet confuse their experience in mass society with the experience of the masses. These people are provided with feedback and self-system models in their socialization experience, but for undergraduate students, in such a medium, symbolic interaction has little payoff for one's own self.

The Sociology of Knowledge

A basic assumption of the sociology of knowledge is that ways of feeling, thinking, and acting vary with one's position in the social structure (Mannheim, 1936, p. 125–126). In a rationally organized LSO, feeling, thinking, and acting are too unpredictable. Much of the object of interfacing computer technology with productive and distributive technology is to eliminate human thinking, neutralize human feeling, and minimize human behavioral input. Under these conditions of social organization, consciousness and ideology become divorced from position in the organization—not in the tragic sense, but in the rational sense.

It is not that there is false consciousness, but rather that there is no consciousness of self, no consciousness of being in hostile contrast to others in the LSO, no possibility to develop a special interest and ideology. We are all equally oblivious to the dealings of the LSOs which touch our lives so lightly and so little taken one at a time. How can we develop an ideological orientation to Campbell Soups, International Minerals, Transworld Airlines, U.S. Gypsum, Bell and Howell, or Eastern Kodak? What is the hostile contrast (or benevolent) which Gillette, National Cash Register, or Polaroid bears to one or to one's interest? We can rage at Con Edison, Dow Chemical, or Hershey candy bar, but if our anger exists it can be rationally controlled. Dow stops producing Napalm; Con Edison hires a Madison Avenue firm; or Hershey runs beautiful ads, and we are left alone with our rage.

If one owns 50 shares of Bell Telephone, there is no sense of self involved. The stock is in a mutual fund or a retirement fund and one doesn't even know of his position in the social order. If one purchases Crest toothpaste, one doesn't know whether it is produced by Lever Brothers or by Goodrich, given the corporate conglomerates of the day. If one mines ore or sells tickets, one has so many clients and so many intermediaries that one cannot sort out one's differences and likenesses to those with which one deals. Under these conditions, the relation between position in the social order and consciousness is blurred, traduced, obscured, and finally escapes us. Even the most astute and knowledgeable analyst cannot clarify the relationships we bear to others *vis à vis* complex organizations. Still less can the average man be conscious of these relationships. Ralph Nader has done much to restore our consciousness of relatedness to large-scale establishments in the market-place. He, together with the ecologists and environmentalists, has conveyed some sense of the hostile contrast to which these establishments generally stand in respect to the general public. The message is reaching the people who are not touched by Domhoff, Marcuse, Brown, Fromm, and other critics whose audience is limited to college students and some intellectuals.

In a simpler society, one's enemies were ancient enemies, fixed and fixable in time and space, and tied to particular persons and particular interests. Now, large-scale organizations have no particular geographical location, no time span, no permanent population base. One cannot find them, cannot respect them, cannot hate them, cannot identify them. In that one does not experience the LSO, the LSO cannot shape one's consciousness. In that one cannot know one's relation to a given LSO, one cannot form a stable orientation to others involved in the LSO.

Language and Self

As more and more information is generated and transmitted by technology in language systems unknown to the persons who are the subjects of that information, the historic linkage between self and symbols becomes diminished.

Marx (1845) has stated that:

> Language is as old as consciousness; language is practical consciousness, as it exists for other men, and thus as it first really exists for myself as well. Language, like consciousness, only arises from the need, the necessity, of intercourse with other men. ... Consciousness is therefore from the very beginning a social product, and remains so as long as men exist at all. (Bottomore, 1964, pp. 19–20)

But as social communications come to involve language forms and media divorced from the consciousness of particular men, then social systems can get along without that component of the self-structure conventionally labeled "consciousness."

A particular case can be seen in the use of computers to decode, store, retrieve, encode, and transfer information. Libraries are the archaic form of impersonal consciousness. Computer technology finishes the process of separating man from social language systems, hence societal (but not private) consciousness. Even in libraries, people are necessary to read, interpret, and respond to the information contained therein. Computer technology can be used to eliminate people in the flow of information for any given cybernetic control system; and cybernetic control systems are the key to the question of structure generation and elaboration in all systems, social or otherwise.

One must understand that the point here is not the end of language but rather the beginning of the separation of language into two types: one having great relevance for social systems and little relevance for self-systems (Fortran, Cobol, and such), and the second type having great relevance for the self-system but progressively less for the social system (Esperanto, English, Russian, Chinese, French, etc.).

Other than the fact that there are new language forms used to generate social systems and that they have very little relevance to the self-system of those who are the subject of the information contained in computer language systems, there are other reasons why the language systems of large-scale organizations do not affect the shape of self.

If the receiver of communication is another computer rather than an individual, then all that Burke (1950) has said about language as a source of cooperation, of motives, of identification between self and others is invalid. It is not that data flow from computers *could not* motivate us by manipulating symbols, but that they *do not* motivate us since we are not linked to that data flow.

For the purposes of large-scale organizations, it is not necessary to include in computer languages symbols expressing the grand sweep of history, the symbolic content of dreams, or the lessons contained in fables and myths. These are necessary to the socialization process and to the organization of human behavior, as Freud, Simmel, Mead, and Duncan would stress, but such symbols are not necessary to the tasks of computers, machinery, and other electronic machines. The questions of motivation, purpose, and maintenance are solved differently for the technotronic system than for the operating self-system. Conversation is, as Simmel says, "the most general vehicle for all that men have in common," but in large-scale organization very little of the communication takes the *form* of conversation. In LSOs the points of information exchange are not beliefs and matters of conscience, as in the case of religious symbols; nor are they causes and positions of interest to large-scale organization as they are in political dialogues and when attesting to one's ideals and loyalties in discourses—all of these deeply affect the nature of self in human language systems. However, the point of information flow in computer systems as they attend to LSO affairs is shipping orders, subscriptions, costs, inventories, lists, locations, etc. One cannot build an adequate self out of flat and spiritless language. The language of business, finance, commerce, and politics is not the language of spirited human beings.

Computer language systems can be more precise and predictable than human language systems. Any LSO seeking to extend control over its internal and external environments benefits from the replacement of humans by machines. It is again a functional advantage to dissever self from the social system in large-scale organizations. To the extent that LSOs represent the major organization feature of a society, language and consciousness become separable from self.

ROLE MODELS

James Baldwin (1895) has written that there is no dichotomy between self and society. The individual and the group are part of each other; that linkage is realized:

> by taking in "copies" from the world and the world is enabled to set higher copies only through the constant reactions of the individual self upon it. Morally I am as much a part of society as physically I am a part of the world's fauna; and as my body

gets its best explanation from the point of view of its place in a zoological scale, so morally I occupy a place in the social order; and an important factor in the understanding of me is the understanding of it. (cited in Martindale, 1960, p. 316)

But one must ask where, in large-scale organizations, there is a role model to serve as blueprint for self-structure for the masses. The answer is "nowhere." There is a stable expectation levied on an individual by the societal system, but that expectation does not bear upon any part of the self which answers to the question, "Who am I?"

To buy toothpaste from Colgate is a firmly held and expertly expressed expectation of that LSO. Most people buy that toothpaste without reference to the question of whether they have a personal investment in Colgate. Buying toothpaste is role-related behavior but not related to the role structure of the LSO in question. Only were it related to the task of generating self out of the role differentiations *of the large*-scale establishment would the purchase of toothpaste have meaning to the transfer of the roles in *that* organization to the self-structure for *that* purchaser.

SOCIAL CONTROL AND SELF-STRUCTURE

The means for keeping persons uptight to the normative structure of specific role takes in folk societies is complex, efficacious, and ubiquitous. In short take systems, there is little policing and no need for sanctioning. General Motors cannot sanction, negatively, those persons who do not organize their behavior in ways compatible with this social take. General Mills cannot support a policing system which checks whether one stocks Wheaties in one's cupboard. General Foods could not establish economically a court system by which nonconformers are degraded and sentenced. As wealthy as is General Dynamics, it could scarcely afford to establish the segregation facilities for the "resocialization" of "deviants."

The exciting implication of this perspective is that one sees the end of crime and punishment. The mechanics for second line social control become too cumbersome as a LSO becomes the standard unit of social organization in post*Gesellschaft* and short takes become the typical unit of experience. The rhetoric of "deviance" is irrational in the marketing and servicing strategy of such a social system.

An increasingly large portion of society in post*Gesellschaft* foregoes the tactic of gaining structure by defining nonconformity as "crime." How much of that which remains will continue to obtain order by the use of the technique of pronouncing crimes and policing "deviance" is an open question. I return to it in the last chapter in the section on the theory and practice of corruption.

ADVERTISING AND MOTIVATION IN A SHORT TAKE SOCIETY

In a short take society, self ceases to mediate all unit acts by means of the cybernetic process discussed in Chapter 3. The strategy of advertising replaces the self as the mediating structure with psychological imperatives. Status, masculinity, wifehood, fatherhood, citizenship continue to be used as the basis of motivation. However, two developments in mass merchandising are reducing the relevance of selfhood to behavior; and, above all, it is specific kinds of behavior in the marketplace and in public which LSOs must generate in order to survive.

The first development is that of depth psychology, the fundamental assumption of which is that it is better to circumvent the self as the mediator of behavior and go directly to the depths of the unconscious. Thus, many advertising strategies assume a psychological dynamic exists which can be tapped to sell soap, cigarettes, shaving cream, soup, beer, razor blades, etc. (Dichter, 1964).

One shaving cream commercial assumes that most of us are still immature in psychosexual terms. It purports to take advantage of our presumed latent homosexuality which in turn derives from an unresolved Oedipal complex. The ad presents an effeminate male approaching carefully an older man in front of a fruit stand while smearing the face of the older man with shaving cream. The older man, in turn, ejaculates in the protagonist's hand thereby providing the semblance if not the substance of manhood.

Another ad for razor blades attempts to take advantage of the assumption most men have vestiges of castration anxiety by including a huge razor which is worshipped by those in terror of it. A beer ad shows solidarity and *Gemutlichkeit* in its exclusively male assemblages drinking "dickie pee-pee."

For women, similar ads assume hidden needs and similar inability to resist the appeal. Some ads play on the hostility of daughter to mother by staging the triumph of the daughter over the mother in the relatively safe arenas of childrearing (better medicine, better diapers, better baby food), clothing, cookery, cleaning, and shopping. Some ads touch more dangerous themes by dealing with penis envy and lesbianism, especially ads for cigarettes and household cleansers.

Children are subject to the same approach, which ties products to childhood anxieties—acceptance, image, parental love, etc. Many ads sell toys for aggression, destruction, violence, and retaliation. Cereal ads seem to tie purchase to anxiety about the degree to which mother loves the child. The cereal in question is essential and should not be denied to the child.

One gasoline ad had eight or so symbolic representations of the primal scene: a can of oil is punctured by a sharp pointed penis surrogate; a vacuum cleaner sucks ashes out of a dirty ashtray; a nozzle is thrust into a gas tank; a dip stick is carefully wiped clean and stuck back into its hole; a battery is filled, hole by hole, by a pointed syringe; and so on. The sequence and the camera angles are quite emphatic about the sexual nature of a stop at the friendly neighborhood gas station.

In addition to the advent of depth psychology and its deliberate exclusion of self, there is the development that goods should be purchased on their technical merits rather than upon their connection with tribal, national, sexual, or age-graded differentiations. Again, inasmuch as these differentiations have been, historically, the social structural supports of self, to eliminate these considerations is to eliminate some of self. Twenty years ago, one did not buy a Volkswagen since it had ethnic connections alien to one's own self-structure. The same has been true for Japanese products, Italian food, Soviet ideas, and Chinese values. Modern advertising cannot tie its merchandising efforts to narrowly based populations. It cannot deal in self-systems and maximize sales. The ad industry has, in the rational pursuit of its goals, furthered the separation of society from self.

Differentiation and the Set of Social Identities

In a folk society, there are but a scarce half dozen or so differentiations. Under this condition of social organization, it is possible to use the self-system as the repository of ordered behaviors. As society becomes highly differentiated, there develops so many social takes and associated identities that it is technically impossible to fit them all into the same self-structure.

The temporary solution is, of course, to use different sets of persons among whom to parcel out separate sets of social identities. Thus, among 2000 persons in a community, one might find several weavers, herders, smiths, sanders, saddlers, millers, mayors, harpers, griffins, enwrights, cartwrights, wheelwrights, and assorted fishers, wickmen, whitings, walters, and Trujillos.

But this solution is awkward in the extreme for large-scale organizations. To remain mapped to a changing environment, it is necessary to change role structure continuously. Therefore it becomes dysfunctional to tie occupational identities to any one man's life. To do so would require that the person be discarded along with the role, or that it be necessary to "retrain" the individual and provide him with psychiatric care for the harm done, thereby, to the self-system. But there is a point of diminishing returns after socializing people to the $N + 1$th social identity. How many social identities one self-system can support is not established. I think 10 to 20 such social indentities constitute the upper limits, since self cannot exist unless it is experienced. It becomes progressively difficult to experience any given identity with the addition of the Nth identity. Perhaps the optimum number of social identities in a self-system is one strong and clearly known one. As the half-life of information decreases from 1000 years to 5 years or less, even the present stability of social differentiation vanishes and with it vanishes the self-system which depends upon the social statuses in that differentiation.

PROCESSUAL DISCONTINUITY AND SELF-STRUCTURE

One cannot escape one's self structure. In a long take society, one's self-structure is laden with 3 to 20 or more social identities. These identities are expected to organize one's behavior in continuous fashion. Thus, one cannot escape being a male, a Catholic, a warrior, or whatever. The social processes which generate those associated social structures have an historical record; they are continuous, and they are bound to time and place. Wherever one is, there also is the social structure.

In short take societies, role involvements are episodic, ahistorical, non-temporal, and nonspatial.* One may move into a short take without any historical antecedents: for example, "I am a visitor to Ghana." One may take a short role episodically: "I am a fan of the Detroit Lions,"—a take which recurs weekly. One may be involved in a social take which has no geography nor time-boundedness: for example, "I am an advocate of peace."

Under the condition of discontinuity in time, in history, and in space, it is most difficult to tie self to social process. "What am I between takes?" is the rhetorical question. The answer is not rhetorical; it is given preliminary form in Chapter 6. In folk societies there is little discontinuity in social process, so tying self to social order produces stability of behavior and security of mind. In societies with great processual discontinuity, much mischief is done to self if social discontinuity also means self-discontinuity.

RITES OF PASSAGE

One of the central mechanisms used in folk societies in order to harness the self-system to the social is the rite of passage. Van Gennep (1966), has examined the theme of rites of passage and has preempted the field. Not only did Van Gannep delineate the phases common to rites of passage (separation, transition, and incorporation) but he focused upon the social function of such rites; he expressed the movement from one social status to another as an "opening of doors."

---

*This idea first developed in 1962 in a seminar with Professor Edward Rose.

But more important than the incorporation of the individual into the social structure, a rite of passage incorporates the social structure into the individual self-system. The rite of naming awards the child with a term suggesting some social differentiation: male-female, age cohort, kin sib, clan, secret society, etc. (Van Gennep, p. 62). At one and the same time, the name suggests how others are to levy expectations upon the person *and* how the person is to organize his own behavior: thus are systems of regularized social patterns achieved in folk societies. In complex LSOs, names do not organize behavior nor do they differentiate expectations levied. Names can be converted to numbers since all clients are treated the same, or nearly so. The Bell Telephone System does not relate differently to the millers than to the wheelers; the expectations are standard.

I went to an ROTC commissioning ceremony recently and observed the transferral of social status to self-system. There was a duly authorized agent of society (the main speaker) who legitimized the transferral; a priestly intermediary who gave, by proxy, the sacred sanction; an oath of fealty to the office was administered, optionally by a friend or functionary; a presentation of commissions by that speaker (the more celebrated, the better); and the enveloping milieu of wives, mothers, children, as well as one bemused professor. Total institutions, such as the military, are able to spend time to obliterate existing social identities, to socialize new ones, and offer the rite of passage as the central means for generating the sociology of it all. Garfinkel (1956) and Goffman (1961) discuss the processes involved in tying self to society in totalistic systems and it is most involved but follows the patterns above.

This is the point: in order to process masses of persons through the social system, it is not rational to create bottlenecks at either portal—entrance or exit (Young, 1968). Rites of passage are not used in LSO *for the masses*. Face rights require little more than mere presence or, at most, a ticket. Here it is possible to see that the ticket replaces the self-system component as the means by which to construct the system out of the behavior of some part of the population. In the concrete instance, a person presents a ticket and recognition to participate in a given line of activity ensues. One can be involved in any number of marketplace activities by checking in or out with some pass or another. In a folk society, wherein the primary requirement is a given social identity, one is foreclosed from involvement unless all concerned others are assured one is the right sort of person.

In the Catholic Church, where the social identity is a permanent feature of both self and social order, there is no such checking and granting of face rights. One is assumed to always *be* a Catholic. In the services of some other churches, one is greeted, welcomed, escorted, introduced, and seated, all activity made necessary only by virtue of the fact that membership cannot be taken for granted. The Baptist Church cannot assume that everyone at its services *is* as a matter of course a Baptist. For that reason, recognition routines exist by which to legitimate face engagements on a temporary basis until such time as membership is formally bestowed by rites of passage. And since self is not continued after the service, one finds disengagement routines at the end of many Protestant services. Not so with the Catholic service; there is a closing routine but it is not meant to sever self from social order until next Sunday.

The point is, to repeat, that such recognition and disengagement routines create bottlenecks at the beginning and end of face engagements. The rational solution is to abbreviate both or find some rapid alternative for checking on legitimacy of involvement.

SOLIDARITY

In folk societies, in order to generate a social system in some real, phenomenological way, persons typically are put through a routine by which common feelings, common cognitive orientations, and reciprocal behavior replace private feelings, idiosyncratic cognitive orientations, and nongame behavior. To achieve this extraordinary feat, several mechanisms are used. For example, in church services at time 1, one might observe 60 different cognitive orientations, 20 different moods, and nongame (from the perspective of any given normative map) behavior. Suddenly an organ inveighs its mighty tones and the 60 different cognitive orientations fall away and are replaced by one shared definition of the situation. Light moods, gay moods, lustful moods, indifferent moods, friendly moods are in a moment swept away and replaced by awe, reverence, and humility: shared. Persons may be observed to stand as one, speak as one, kneel as one, pray as one, sing as one, and be seated as one. There can be no greater solidarity than in that group where everyone feels the same, takes the same cognitive orientation, and exhibits the same behavior.

For the religious services I have observed, the generation of solidarity takes from 5 to 20 minutes out of the schedule of the system. It is most efficacious in differentiating "A" from "Not-A," i.e., "church" from "not-church." But LSOs do not use the psychobiological capacities of people in order to differentiate. LSOs use order blanks and credit cards and sometimes build the differentiation into the architecture, as when one's house is served by a natural gas company and another's is not, or when girls are housed in one dorm and boys in another at a college.

The main point I wish to make is that when the psychobiological capacities of people cease to be used in order to differentiate "A" from "Not-A" in post*Gesellschaft* society, then self is even more divorced from social order. To build the definition of the situation into the architecture of it all, as with wealthy churches, means to relieve humans of the task of generating that part of the social system. A store front church *is* much more a human venture in that a "religious service" cannot emerge on the level of social reality without human input of a most challenging sort. With the customers of the El Paso Natural Gas Company, there is a great rationality and effective transfer of negentropy from environment to system, but little psychobiological input and less solidarity is required. Can a society without psychobehavioral solidarity last? I think so. Whatever the case, a LSO cannot spend time and synergy on generating solidarity while differentiation is already achieved and still be said to be in rational pursuit of system goals.

DISENGAGEMENT ROUTINES

LSOs do offer disengagement routines, but as an exception rather than as a rule. Sometimes in LSOs a person becomes involved emotionally in the throughput phase of engagement. Some pride in self or self-embarrassment has occurred which requires LSOs to allocate some skeletal crew to handle disengagement questions. For example, a clerk offends a customer and a manager mollifies the customer, who can then exit gracefully, his self-respect restored.

The disengagement routines in LSO are compact, efficient, and speedy— the speedier, the more rational, in terms of systems' goals. This is possible in that the self is not used as a means to bind persons into systems. Where the self is so used, it is necessary to have a funeral, a divorce, a court-martial, a degradation ceremony, a hearing, a desecration, excommunication, expulsion, and banishment—a cooling-out process.

Where self is apart from the social, banishment, exile, degradation are nonsense terms. If the Bell Corporation discontinues service to me, I do not take it as a matter of shame, nor do I feel debased: I may be on vacation; I may be moving; I may not want it. Debasement and shame have no place in a yellow-page society. They do not solve any organizational problems of the system and, hence, are "irrational." Sometime in the future, I expect we will cease using the self-system of the "student" as a structural support for the social system in higher education. The first indicator of this transition will be reflected in our grading practices. Although grades are used to shame or to embellish the self-component, were the social self not at stake, grades would be meaningless to the social system. A second indicator will be the termination of "loco parentis." The person, rather than the dean, will be his own master. At that time, to "drop out" will have no individious overtones, and "failing" will cease to be a meaningful term, one does not "fail" when he fails to conform to the expectations of Sears-Roebuck.

THE DRAMATURGICAL SOCIETY

When Goffman's writings first appeared on the scene, established sociologists did not know how to receive them. Surely human behavior is not that cynical, said some. Surely the individual is more a master of his soul, said others. But more innocent students came to appreciate Goffman as one of the most perceptive and valuable observers of the human tableau. Chinoy (1961) mentions Gobineau but not Goffman in his index although *Presentation of Self* came out in 1956 and again in 1959 in more accessible form. Francis Merrill (1961) mentions Cornelius Golightly but not Goffman. Lasswell, Burma, and Aronson (1965) offer Goffman under the rubric of "Interaction and Communication" but ignore his major works in their chapter on personality. Sherif (1969) gives Goffman fair but very brief treatment. Manis and Meltzer (1967) are certain that Goffman is a valuable analyst and note that he focuses mainly on settings containing insiders and outsiders, cadre and clients, front and back regions. His contribution to the genesis and the presentation of self is not discussed.

Under the conditions of social organization which describe contemporary society, a theorist such as Goffman has special relevance. His dramaturgical mode of social analysis presents a useful way of examining a society in which men are not trying to do, but to be, in which a person is evaluated by his appearance. The *Presentation of Self in Everyday Life* (1959) deals with the task of image projection and management of impressions. This presentation must have adequate dramaturgical direction in order to be credible, and this technique is a part of the process of socialization. Instead of viewing this as a "con-game" approach as Cuzzort (1969, p. 173) does in his otherwise excellent treatment of Goffman or as supportive of the sociology of fraud as does Gouldner (1970, p. 384) in his excellent treatise on the sociology of sociology, a better way to begin is by asking under what conditions of social organization is a dramaturgical analysis appropriate. There are several. In a mass society, self is not used as the major social-psychological structural support for the construction of social reality. In order to generate customers, clients, passengers, fans, and such, advertising is used instead of socialization. Needs, urges, and predispositions are generated one at a time. This is in marked contrast to the process of socialization in earlier societies where the constraints of behaviors are assembled in packages (called role-sets in our jargon) and inculcated into the self-system of a neophyte as a "social identity." These social identities are then used as a basis for the organization of behavior in specific situations and mediate needs, urges, proclivities, etc. But socialization is too slow and expensive. In a mass society, the science of psychology is used to circumvent the self-system. Science now is used to link product directly to psychological imperatives such as sex, hunger, curiosity, identity-quest and the like.

In a mass society, one also needs cues from others and needs to watch himself closely if he is going to be able to perform in roles which are short, episodic, ahistorical, and bear no permanent relationship to one's own self-structure. This I call a short take society and view it to be a social condition central to the necessity for dramaturgical handling of one's self and of others. The fact that one is regularly required to transact social meanings with unknown others means that one must allocate some part of his language facilities to the task of communicating just "who" he is at that time and place. Information about the roles one is currently embodying is hung upon clothes, hair, cosmetics, and upon comportment. By these means do we know who is the doctor, the gas station attendant, the clerk, the customer, the chairman, and the janitor.

The norm of anonymity itself is a necessary adjunct to a short take society wherein one goes from one short take to another. Between social takes, one must be accorded civil inattention and permitted to go quickly from one take to another unencumbered by friendly or by hostile overtures. Friendship and crime alike are forbidden to a short take society. This norm of anonymity makes strangers of us all and requires a stable set of visual and behavioral presentments which inform us who is accessible as well as to whom we must accord civil inattention in the public sector of social discourse.*

In a caste society, one need not be too concerned about the management of impressions to others superior in the hierarchy. The bonds which tie serf and landowner, slave and master, peasant and lord are reciprocal and enduring. In contemporary society, the underlings and overlings alike are replaceable and one needs to look to the task of staging a convincing impression of adequacy in the structure of reciprocity. Where there is stratification without permanent bonds, the needs to dissemble, to mask hostility toward powerful others, to adopt proper styles of deference and demeanor, to arrange images and appearances become integral modes of comportment in

---

*There is an excellent discussion of the concepts of civil inattention and accessibility in Goffman (1963, p. 83).

the task of survival. The point is that the best way to understand deceit and dramaturgy is by way of the organization of society rather than in terms of character.

In many societies, the opportunities for exploitation and evasion of reciprocity proliferate as complexity and anonymity increase in spite of a real increase in functional interdependence. Here, it can be seen that the interest of one segment of the population may be so inimical to interests of other segments that it becomes necessary to create deceptive images of the flow of events. An instance of this can be seen in the coverage given to the Santa Barbara oil spill. It was in the interests of the major oil producers not to have all aspects of the problem and the magnitude of the problem reported to the public, and the story was released gradually with many ambiguities. This is an example of what Boorstin refers to as the "creeping event." An event actually takes place, but the manifest signs are "arranged to occur at an inconspicuously gradual and piecemeal pace" (Boorstin, p. 13). In this way, resistance is diffused and some logical consequences of the event may be eliminated. There is a blurring of distinction between the real and the pretend as much of the event becomes managed and staged.

In an organically consolidated society, the synergy of functional interchange is subverted by the power of the corporate state. Parameters of growth, profit, and control of environment on the part of corporate-like entities conflict with the parameters of service, reciprocity, and quality of human life. Part and parcel of the enterprise of controlling its own environment as a corporate goal involves the use of the technology of image construction and control. The dramaturgical arts and crafts lend themselves nicely to such corporate interests.

Mass media has helped to solve the problem of establishing an image. It provides the technology needed to project impressions throughout the society; and as need for a newer, more up-to-date image arises, in a very short time span mass media makes it possible to replace an image that is no longer serviceable. A vast cadre of artists, poets, scenarists, camera men, producers, writers, editors, engineers, publicists and such have provided the world of reality with a corps of experts from the world of make believe. In an impoverished society, kings and popes hold a virtual monopoly over services of the managers of illusion and pretend. In an affluent society, every one can subscribe to the forms of art as well as theatre and the monopoly over staging and drama maintained by church and by state disappears.

Under contemporary conditions of theatrical technology, it is possible for this cadre to create what Boorstin terms the "pseudo-event" in which "conditions are arranged to simulate a certain kind of event, such that certain prearranged conditions follow as though the actual event had taken place" (Boorstin, p. 12). Pseudo-events often result from the public demand for "news." Commentators and reporters must fill every hourly broadcast and every daily paper by manufacturing or managing events. Events may even be scheduled beforehand and rehearsed, as are the interviews in *Playboy* and *Psychology Today*. News is constructed much as a theatrical script is written and performed.

In medieval Europe, artists and artisans were concerned with religious themes in paintings, tapestries, philosophy, drama, and music. Artists and artisans created furnishings, fixtures, halls, palaces, cabinets, tables, silver, coin, and ceramics to serve, exalt, and comfort the nobility of church, state, and commerce. Now the best artists and craftsmen ply their trade in the world of advertising and entertainment. A full blown industry in the enterprise of image making is indispensible to a dramaturgical society.

When products are standardized, the market for imaginary differences on which to sell a commodity is created. Image makers become a recognized group of specialists. As Gouldner sees it, "Dramaturgy marks the transition from an older economy centered on production to a new one centered on mass marketing and promotion, including the marketing of the self" (1970, p. 381). This marketing of the self, resulting from changes in the social organization of interaction is a main feature of contemporary society. It originates with the fact that interaction frequently occurs among anonymous others who are known to each other only by subtle handlings of dress, comportment, and cosmetics as a means to signal how we differ from each other sociologically. In a folk society, in primary groups, we know each other cognitively and personally. In a standardized society, staffed by replaceable people, we seldom learn enough about most others to recognize a given individual cognitively. Thus, anonymous others must stage their presentments in order that we know to whom, among unknown others, we must grant face rights and how, in the changing episodes of social encounters, we must respond to the occasion.

As far as commodities other than the self are concerned, the advent of mass production coupled with industrial espionage has diminished the differences between products. The artisans of imagery create and magnify differences between products largely replaceable. Aspirin is sold on the basis of differences in rates of dissolving. Cars are sold on the basis of differences in windshield wipers. Air travel is sold on the basis of leg room. Detergents are sold on the basis of non-existent psychosexual meaning. Bread is sold on the basis of wrappings. Shoes are sold on the basis of color differences. Wine and beer vary chiefly with respect to the shape of the bottle. Food is sold on the basis of differences in trade names as are washers, dryers, refrigerators, and carpeting. Often the product is made in the same factory and the trade label applied just before shipment to the retailer.

Pricing agreements, area franchises, industry-wide union pacts, marketing arrangements, fair trade laws, licensing and patenting practices, as well as supplier monopolies contribute to the standardization of form, content, and conditions of production, distribution, and retail. Such conditions contribute enormously to the dramaturgical approach to social enterprise. As Gouldner (1970, p. 381) emphasizes, a market for illusion choice is created when the range of real choices open to a given segment of society is restricted. There is no news, so news is manufactured; there is no choice, so the illusion of choice must be created.

After Marx, social psychology has two turning points: one is Mead and the other is Goffman. Mead is the first to show us the mechanics by which self is called forth. By 1968, Cuzzort is able to leave to Goffman the crucial chapter on symbolic interaction and the organization of behavior. Mead is reduced to a footnote on page 176 and Goffman is "the" analyst. I do not regard this as an either/or question; both Mead and Goffman are necessary. Mead represents to us the development of self in a society where long takes ensure the continued and permanent presentation of self in society. Goffman represents to us the enactment of short take social roles involving the management of impression and of personal or team front. For Mead, self and society *are* twinborn; for Goffman, self and society are assembled together but the social take is not taken home. The individual follows the script, but when the "play" is over, he is no longer one of those things and leaves. He is not "conning" anyone and his behavior is not cynical. It is simply that the structure of society has changed in the last 30 years and new theoretical perspectives are required to handle the data.

SUMMARY

In this chapter, I have tried to think through all the major ways in which society might be said to create and to make use of the self-system. I have attempted to show that these ways are not used in LSOs—not because LSOs are inhuman monstrosities, but because to use the self-system as a means to generate LSO is neither necessary nor efficient.

To be sure, human behavior is vital to the operation of the LSO, but not that behavior keying off a social identity reflected in *both* self and social order simultaneously. The behavior is there and the social role is there and the social identity is there, but the social role is a short take and does not get transferred into the self-system *via* a rite of passage. The individual moves into and out of the social take with little permanent consequence for self-structure or negative consequence for social stability. There are other, more rational ways to gain stability and ultrastability in a LSO.

In the final chapters, we must try to understand more human ways to build a self-system that does not depend upon LSO involvement, as well as ways which increase the probability that persons will turn on their psycho-biological capacities to think, to generalize, to extrapolate, to integrate, to decode, retrieve, transpose, to feel rage, warmth, intimacy, joy, pain and awe, wonder and despair, hope and hate, to leap, to strike, to turn, to love, to move away, and to move toward. We must seek after the new sources of self, the new components of self, and inquire as to more human uses of self.

CHAPTER 6

New Sources of Self*

COMPUTER TECHNOLOGY AND THE SHRINKING MIDDLE CLASS CADRE

Social system components are linked by information flow rather than by the mechanical, chemical, and electromagnetic bonds of physical systems. The more rational and foolproof the information media, codes, and receiving apparatus, the better organized the social system. Industrial technology gave the middle class affluence as well as a vital part in the cybernetic control of information flow. Computer technology takes away the cybernetic control function of middle management. Their children shall inherit the service enterprises of law, medicine, science, arts, and leisure. Some of their children. Many of the children of affluent society will not be able to find positions in the occupational structure by which to give meaning and challenge to their human capacities. Rather than to be nonhuman and to lead the plastic life of Mum&Dad&Buddy&Sis, many of these children will turn on human capacities in private ways. The same is true at the other end of the population pyramid. As the age of "retirement" lowers, the divorce between population and LSO increases and the percentage of the population which acts as cadre to the LSO shrinks and, as it shrinks, the role of formal society in supporting self shrinks.

As long as information exchange was in the biologic age, social systems had to put up with the frailties of an animated entity. The mechanical age of information flow required the interface of biology with hardware; the Technetronic Age (Brzezinski, 1968) successfully and progressively eliminated the biological interface in most areas. This changes the validity of the Marxian assumption that the world of work is the central source and use of self. In this chapter, I should like to give some ideas of the new sources and uses of self.

*With the assistance of David Schnell and Charles Brown.

The reader should understand that when I theorize that self is privately constructed and privately used, I mean something quite technical: I do not mean to say that self arises without social structural supports. I mean, in the first instance, that a person has the option of which of many social systems (e.g., universities, libraries, books, television, plays, theatre, movies and any other) to turn to in order to select elements to incorporate into his self-system. In the second and most important instance, I mean to say that the content of self is private to the individual. The *pattern* for the self will be unique to the individual concerned under this mode of self-actualization. The traditional process of socialization presents to the individual ready-made and standardized components for the self-system which are identical for those who precede and for those who succeed him. The private use of social structures for self-organizing is new to the experience of the species and is cause for concern and for alarm also.

In this connection, theorist and layman alike should understand that the private development of self derives from the fact that transactions within a LSO will not be designed in such a way that a particular social identity will be inculcated into a particular self-system *via* socialization routines. In the past, for example in the army, involvement meant becoming a private first-class, a sergeant, a major, a colonel. The same is true for hospitals, prisons, and occupations; the end product of involvement is the associated social identity— patients and doctors, cons and screws, welders and foremen. Rather than a given social identity as the payoff for involvement, a social identity which derives from the organization of social system, the payoff for such involvement is now of much less consequence to the self-system—perhaps of no consequence at all. When one goes to a supermarket, one does not have to "have" a given self in order to have face rights in the legitimate line of action; one has but to "present" oneself as a customer. Thus interaction has little or no payoff for self-structure. A disembodied voice over the phone, or a written order, is accepted on its face value and does not require an extensive probing of the self to verify that the self-structure is appropriate to some given, known model of what people who deal with the store should *be* like.

All social identities in the self-system become irrelevant to the structure of action in post*Gesellschaft*. There is a social identity in the table of organization of the supermarket around which one must organize one's behavior: i.e., that of "customer." But the critical point to focus upon is that the social identity is *external* to the self-system. It is a social identity around which to manage one's front for a short time and to then discard. It never enters the self-system as a permanent part of the individual self-system which answers the question, "Who am I?"

The general point here is that the supermarket has alternate means to generate system without the use of a person's self-structure. This means that if interaction in the system has some permanent payoff for self (I am going to buy this commodity in order to "put it together") then that payoff is private to the individual in question and not to the role structure of the supermarket *qua* supermarket. The structure of the private self is not patterned by the table of organization of the market. Although some behavior might well be patterned, one should not confuse behavior with self.

As theorist and layman understand the relationship between social structure and self-structure, and the growing discontinuity between the two, it becomes possible to understand the experiments in private self-organization, possible to accept them and possible to facilitate them. The present stance of most theorists varies from bemusement to unconcern; that of laymen varies from indifference to hostility and oppression. The reader should move toward the next sections and consider them in terms of the foregoing rather than as mere cultic movements peopled by "weirdos" and "failures." As with all experiments, most will fail; most will have but a vague vision of purpose. Some will fail to foster the development of self, the experience of life, and will fail to advance the limits of human compassion, warmth, intimacy, and contact. This is to be expected. The point is to maximize the human condition, rather than deny it and we do deny it when we reject out of hand experiments in the creation of new sources of self. We also reject the future in as much as a new model of man is necessary if we are to have a future as human beings.

THE UNDERGROUND CHURCH AS A SOURCE OF SELF*

Robert Theobald has said, somewhere, that a religious revival is in progress whose potential can be perceived only dimly. Malcolm Boyd, formerly of the campus ministry at Colorado State University, is one of the harbingers of that movement. In his prayers, psalms, plays, and poetry, Boyd (1968) has stimulated a more personal orientation to religion, a more human use. Boyd insists that instead of "running" with the commercial establishment only at Christmas, Jesus run with you and me for a while, stressing the "me" rather than the worker, the parent, the citizen. God is used currently in American society to help us drive safely, get to work regularly, win football games and a war now and then. This is true if one goes by the content of the established churches; in the underground church, the self is the focus of loving attention.

People are running from the established church services which mold them to public, social, and fiscal respectability; people are much too full of life to

---

*This section written with the aid of Charles Brown.

accept that. They are running to religiously-oriented (but mixed) communes, to underground churches, to encounter groups which focus upon the meaning and ends of life, seminars in Zen and Tao (which are very personal religions), coffee house ministries—and they are taking Jesus with them. Some people are trying to stay within the regular church and to revivify it by new worship forms, including guerrilla theatre, rock masses, and sociodrama. The God of the established society is dying and the God of private man is coming to birth in this movement.

The social use of religion increases as God is taken into the productive process in medieval times and into the distributive process in Protestant times. At some point in time technology renders Godly concern with production and capital formation unnecessary and God can turn his attention to consumption. I think this means a private use of God similar to that of pre-capitalistic times.

The expression "underground church" is probably a misnomer and, at best, misleading. The meetings of members of the underground church, while seldom publicized, are almost never kept a carefully guarded secret. Leading members appear to engage in limited, although circumspect, proselytizing. It also appears that many church authorities are aware of the existence of underground communities within their own territories, but so far have refrained from any official action designed to suppress them. An example of this is the visit paid by the Archbishop of Sante Fe, New Mexico to an underground community located in Albuquerque, New Mexico during the summer of 1968.

The underground church can perhaps be defined as a parallel religious structure arising from the ribs of the institutional church and expressing the need of adherents of the movement for personal involvement with others in a shared faith by bypassing official Church structures and leadership, which are perceived as an obstacle to personal involvement.

When asked why he became involved in the underground church, one former Catholic priest responded: "There is a coldness and lack of personalism in the institutional church. Organization takes precedence over organism. It has an obsession with past traditions: marriage laws, external forms of confessions, birth control, and celibacy. Creativity and imagination are pushed into *last* place."

Expressed in these words is a summary of the reasons given by almost all the members of the underground church who were asked this same question in the last year.* Taken as a whole, the reasons given express a dissatisfaction on the part of a growing number of church members with some of the structural components of their church systems. This dissatisfaction, and the consequent search for alternatives, centers around those structural components which are perceived as hindering, if not actually preventing, individuals from realizing and expressing themselves as distinct human persons with individual needs and desires, searching for personal, primary relationships with other distinct human persons. The main element that appears to be common to the members of various "communities" known as the underground church is the shared feeling that the institutional churches depersonalize their members and reduce them all to the least common denominator. Whether institutionalized churches indeed function as a depersonalizing agent may be problematic; that they are perceived in this way by a significant number of people, evidenced by the phenomenon of the underground church, is a social fact.

What is most dramatically revealing about the nature of the underground church is the gathering of the members for their religious service, usually referred to as the liturgy. This consists usually, in Catholic groups when a priest is present, of a gathering in the home of one of the members. Singing and scripture readings selected for their appropriateness to the particular occasion ordinarily precede the Eucharistic celebration. Sometimes readings of poetry or fiction or selections from newspapers are substituted for scripture readings. In place of the usual sermon a dialogue among the members may take place, during which members may express their interpretation of the readings or their application of the readings to the needs and problems of those present. The celebration of the Eucharist is led by the priest, who usually does without the vestments and liturgical vessels required by the institutional church. The structure of this part of the liturgy is quite "loose," as it is for the entire service, permitting, and even encouraging, spontaneity. The service usually concludes with the participants embracing, and a social event including visiting, singing, and food.

The relationship between the phenomenon of the underground church and the individual's search for self should be quite evident. That the self emerges from one's relationships in primary groups has been so well-established as to be a cliché. The institutionalized church has become in many respects a large-scale organization. Contacts between members characteristically are of a secondary nature. Church services often consist of highly formalized ritual, even when the ritual is not elaborate, so that the interaction among members rarely consists of more than physical proximity and the effort

---

*Charles Brown has written a dissertation using the "underground" church as a source of data to test some hypotheses deriving from modern systems theory relative to a theory of parallel social structures under my direction as his Chairman. *The Underground Church and Modern Systems Theory*, 1970, unpublished, Colorado State University.

expended to recite prayers and sing hymns together. Even the greeting exchanged between the minister and the members at the door of the church is usually formalized and devoid of personal content, and the relationship is rarely that of person to person, but rather role to role. The size of the population of most parishes is often so large that no member can know all the other members and the minister can relate to many of the members only in a tertiary manner; i.e., he provides a service, without ever realizing for whom the service is provided.

The underground church, then, has become for some people a new source of self. Here they find the primary relationships which can provide them with support for ideas, attitudes, values. Here they find people, not an abstract institution, to which they can be committed. Here they find the opportunity, if not the necessity, to involve their selves in the creation and maintenance of community as a social system. And here they find their selves as the center of experience, not the rules governing the "proper" performance of a formalized liturgy. It is the underground church, not the institutional church, which assures its members that they are indeed unique, and which is structured to produce a meaningful self for the individual.

If the organized church invests its energy in servicing social systems in which men can find nothing personal or private then churches will be "liberated" along with the universities or, failing that, parallel structures of the sort mentioned above will thrive. When self and society are twinborn, then the pastor to the social system is pastor to the self-system. As society becomes independent of the self-system and as the pastorate gravitates to the source of money and power, then a truly religious person must find his pastor elsewhere, or, perchance, become his own pastor. The historical mission of religion has been, among other missions, to provide one with a viable social self. One which organizes one's behavior in holistic ways but in relation to one's fellow man as well.

The underground church includes more than those operating on the fringes of established religious denominations. In the larger sense of religious endeavor, there is a new, rich religious orientation developing among the young dropouts from established society. If the Golden Rule of the past was: "Do unto others that which you would have others do unto you," the Ten Commandments together with Deuteronomy directed the application of that rule to primarily social purposes: family, friends, work, politics, and so on. The new commandments developing today direct the application of that Golden Rule to more personal ends. These commandments form sort of a Turing machine which spins out private self-systems in infinite array but which, taken together, produce a gentler generation.

The Commandments*
  1. Be up front.
  2. Put it together with style.
  3. Do your own thing.
  4. Go with the flow.
  5. Feed the hungry bee, if one has the strength.
  6. It's done with people.
  7. It's done with love.
  8. Things that are pleasurable tend to be good.
  9. Be in tune with Nature.
 10. Ecstasy is the way to know Him/Her/It/?
 11. Truth has a small *t*.
 12. Change through personal example.
 13. Experience yourself.

The new religion may be a sturdy source of self. It may take many forms but will share in common the provision of elements by which individuals can compose their own self-system in ways which turn on their psychophysiological capacities to be human. A religion focused on the private life is a better religion than one which is handmaiden to politics, war, and education. One must note that the potential of religion for constraining the impersonal violence of large-scale organizations is yet to be felt in systematic ways. Inasmuch as the family and tribe were the typical unit of organization and experience in biblical times, it is understandable that so little thought is given to the constraint of such establishments by religious parameters except in the disavowal of concern with that which is Caesar's. If religion has to do with the continuing formulation of values by which to live, then there is great need to revitalize politics, education, and business with religious purposes and practices. This can be profitable if a narrow dogmatism based upon tribal myths and upon metaphysical superstitions can be avoided.

THE FREAK COMMUNITY AS *NEO-GEMEINSCHAFT*†

Societies, like all systems, evolve in order to adapt to their environment as it changes, or they cease to exist. It is our opinion that a more complete model for this evolution is *Gemeinschaft* to *Gesellschaft* to complex *Gesellschaft* to neo-*Gemeinschaft*. This is an evolution from a peasant, pre-industrial

---

*Some from Ken Kesey, some from David Schnell, some from R. D. Laing.

†David Schnell wrote his M.A. thesis on the Freak Community, from which much of this material is taken, under my direction as Chairman. *Sources of Self and a Neo-Gemeinschaft Community*, 1969, unpublished, Colorado State University.

culture to an industrial culture to a complex industrial culture characterized not only by industrialization but also by the existence of rapid mass transportation, high geographical mobility, high occupational mobility, the appearance and use of mass media, the dominance of the large-scale organization, and extremely rapid technological innovation, and then evolution to a society containing the features of both peasant and technological societies.

This is, as well, an evolution from cultures which provide for strong structurally supported self-systems that are intimately tied to the social institutions of the culture in order that the individual be a functional part of society, to cultures where there is a separation of self and most of society. In these cultures there is a greater tendency for the self-system to be built around the truncated, short take roles with their limited content together with the alienation associated with inability to direct and orient behavior around those shallow social identities across time and space.

Finally, these cultures evolve, in turn, into cultures where the loss of institutional sources of self is compensated for by noninstitutional sources of self and by the ability to put the self-system to a nonsocietal, private use. It is a central theme of this section that one can view the rise of *neo-Gemeinschaft* cultures as an adaptation to the alienation and selflessness inherent in the complex *Gesellschaft* formation.

In the following pages we will present the characteristics of the *neo-Gemeinschaft* formation and attempt to show how each influences the self-system of an individual involved in this type of culture.

Long Take Roles

Neo-Gemeinschaft is a return to long take roles. The takes are long rather than lifelong. They do not derive exclusively from the social structure as in the case of the old *Gemeinschaft* community. However, occupational roles of the freak community are typically those of the artisan, the craftsman, and the wise man. These roles involve an investment in time during which the individual acquires the knowledge and skill for his occupation. The payoff for this investment is the product that is uniquely that of the individual. This type of occupational role provides an answer to the question of "Who am I?" I am a carpenter; I am a musician; I am a dealer in drugs that bring ecstasy and wisdom; I am a productive member of the community whose product is uniquely mine.

The role of freak is also a long take role, also answering the question of "Who am I?"* One goes through certain rituals and experiences (many of

---

*The term "freak" appears to be devoid of any negative content as used in the commune and in street life.

which are unique to the individual) in order to adopt this role. Once the role is adopted, cues, both visible and external and invisible and internal, give one the knowledge that he is a freak. The identity of freak is a continuing and stable source of self through time and space. It involves numerous stances and beliefs which help the individual organize and direct his behavior in dimensions and directions impossible in short role takes and across many involvements and occasions.

Land and Knowledge as Wealth

The two major sources of wealth within the freak community are land, as in *Gemeinschaft* cultures, and knowledge. Land is highly prized both for its symbolic value as a source of security and its practical value as a source of sustenance. Knowledge, whether it be mystical or practical (how to produce drugs, or take apart and put together a motorcycle), is a source of wealth because it may be traded for other goods and services. Both these sources of wealth are sources of security; they support the individual while he explores the many strange and unsure aspects of himself.

Traditional Knowledge

As in *Gemeinschaft* society, the members of a *neo-Gemeinschaft* culture place a high value on traditional knowledge. In the freak community, the use of astrology and the *I Ching* as methods to explore and explain the universe are quite common. It is not altogether surprising, in a culture based on an ethic of finding out who one is and acting upon this knowledge, that some ready-made answers should be sought. In the freak community the Zodiac identity of Scorpio or Aquarian is legitimate. It is a source of security—one that can easily generate a sense of well-being—to know that there is a plan in the universe and that one has a place in that plan.

Social Relationships

The dominant social relationships of a *neo-Gemeinschaft* society are non-blood kinship, fellowship, and neighborliness. The social entities which arise from these relationships are family units and clan-like or tribal units. The freak community uses love in its broadest possible sense, that of positive affective interaction, as the primary basis for individual and group inter-action. Hostility, when expressed, is generally done so in the form of satire or the put-on (the telling of some improbable story as if it were the truth). Love is a psychological binding mechanism which requires human involvement and human capacities. This is in contrast to a "well organized" large-scale organization which attempts to eliminate the unpredictable and thus the emotional capacities of those involved. The tribal and family units of the freak community use love as a medium of interaction in an attempt to turn on the same psychological capacities which the complex social structure of contemporary American society must turn off in order to operate efficiently.

The freak community can be said to be a *Gemeinschaft* of the mind where a deep commitment to a given set of beliefs forms the basis for a strong social organization. Psychological states are important in the solidarity of this community, in contrast to the contracts which serve as nonpersonal cements used to obtain ordered relationships in *Gesellschaft* cultures.

As one may note from the above, the freak community provides a source of self, as does both *Gemeinschaft* and *Gesellschaft*. The difference is that there is no particular model mirroring in whole or in part the *social* differentiation of the formal organization portion of complex *Gesellschaft*. The point here is to present the freak community as a special case of *neo-Gemeinschaft*, not as the single, exhaustive representative. We expect that, in the future, society will see a division of labor in handling the four generic problems of community organization identified by Knop (1969). Two of the four— mastery (control) of nature and social control—will continue to be handled by complex *Gesellschaft*. Of the other two problems, one, socio-emotional comfort, will be the focus of *neo-Gemeinschaft*. The fourth, socialization, will be the subject of attention of both forms of social organization: complex *Gesellschaft* and *neo-Gemeinschaft*. The task of social control in future society will have to shift from social control of the individual to social control of the LSO. With an adequate self-system, there is little need for policing of private persons. To the degree that *neo-Gemeinschaft* organizations; religions, free universities, encounter groups, freak communities, zodiac, are able to provide people with adequate and satisfying self-systems, to that degree is policing, jurisprudence, and reformation more properly directed at controlling the chaos reigning between large-scale organizations. Face-to-face control is much better for people than mass processing through courts, prisons, and welfare. If a young person could find an adequate source of self in megapolis, the half-savage gangs which roam the streets and the marketplace would be replaced by the love generation. But in the city, there is no source of self for the child: not in family, not in church, not in school, not on television, not in the streets, not in the shops, nor the stores; nowhere is self the subject of attention in complex *Gesellschaft*. In *neo-Gemeinschaft* little other than self is the center of interest and interaction

THE ZODIAC IDENTITIES

Perhaps one of the richest sources of self-system in the future will be the Zodiac. It contains 12 nonsocial differentiations with enough order to organize behavior coherently and enough vagueness to permit variety within that order. We should not shrug off astrology as fad or foible. For many people the *sign* under which they are born becomes a self-fulfilling prophecy in just the same symbolic interactionist way that masculinity or ethnicity become a self-fulfilling prophecy. If one is born under the sign of Gemini, one sees himself as mentally energetic, versatile, witty, and artistic, albeit sometimes fickle and dilettantish. A Virgo becomes discriminating, serving, and methodical, even if picky. As a Capricorn, one is supposed to be steadfast, reserved, traditional, and ambitious, if a little selfish and snobbish.

The *houses* of the Zodiac suggest ways to organize behavior thematically for most of the exigencies of life: honor, friends, troubles, life, riches, relations, home, children, etc. Specific action is suggested or avoided on the basis of conjunctions of the planets. Because there is structure there, one can organize self from Zodiac. Because astrology is institutionalized, it will survive just as the Marine Corps and the Catholic Church survive in that they are institutionalized. Anything with structure can be institutionalized and, if so, can serve as a source of self. There are about 10,000 full-time and 175,000 part-time astrologers (*Time*, 21 March 1969). As computer technology and modern marketing techniques are used, the movement will survive and interest more and more people. The same statement applies to witchcraft, palmistry, numerology, and handwriting analysis. All can and probably will serve as a reservoir out of which to construct self in largely private ways—in part or in whole.

I think the best way to understand the growth and decline of astrology is from the sociological perspective. It offers a source of self when societal sources are changing or diminishing. Whether it reflects celestial necessity, alienation, a product of mass media, or just plain nonsense is open to question. However, there can be no doubt that sun signs organize a lot of self for a lot of people. This has been true in the past and it is true now.

Rationales for Astrology

A great many people "believe" in astrology. The truth value of a particular rationale for the astrological perspective is irrelevant to the sociologist. If people organize their behavior in terms of Zodiac signs, there is a sociological interest. However, some of the rationales are convincing, taken in whole if not in any one part. In this section, I would like to review some common rationales for astrology in order to (1) legitimize the sociological interest in the study of astrology as social structure rather than as fad, and (2) to show how deeply astrology penetrates to every dimension of life activity and to every segment of the population. It is the enormity of the impact of astrology which deserves attention, not the enormity of its factual inaccuracy.

Famous People

Thales, Pythagoras, Anaxagoras, Xeno, and Aristotle are among the luminaries from ancient times who embraced part or all of the assumptions of astrology. Ptolemy was an active advocate of the art. In Imperial Rome, emperors and the wealthy made astrology a focal point around which to plan. St. Augustine and Albertus Magnus agreed that stars had an influence on natural events even if the human will was free. St. Thomas Aquinas apparently shared the same view. Dante worked as if astrology were valid, as did Chaucer and Shakespeare. Cagliostro, Nostradamus, and Caligula leave us a more macabre legacy to join to that of Tycho Brahe and Johannes Kepler. The illustrious mentor of the latter, Copernicus, was said to have held the chair of astrology at Bologna (Naylor, 1967).

The acceptance of astrology depends more upon the ways in which it is legitimated than upon its truth value. The fact that many of the best known names from history can be linked to astrology is well-known to those who seek for rationales even if not known to the nonbeliever. The point here is not that these people accepted astrology but, rather, that since they did so, it is easy for others to rely upon the implied endorsement: it is a powerful endorsement especially when joined with other rationales such as the striking accuracy of prophecy derived from the conjunction and dysjunctions of the stars.

Famous Prophesies

Zechariah prophesied that his son John would be a prophet to the Most High; and John prophesied the advent of the Lord; and Simeon prophesied the salvation of his people. Three wise men saw a star in the East and followed it. And it was prophesied that the son of God came out of Egypt: so did the son of God return from Egypt. Jeremiah prophesied slaughter of the male children and so it was. If one believes in astrology, the Bible is a comfort and a joy to that belief with its prophesies and their connection to the stars.

But if the Bible is not enough, there are a host of other prophesies by which to sustain one's faith. Caesar did not show caution during the Ides of March, and Caesar died. The horoscope of Byzantium predicted its destruction in 1453, and as the Sun passed through Gemini the prophecy was sustained. Henry II fulfilled the prophesy of his death by Nostradamus and Henry's saddened successors saw to it that the Age of Chivalry died with him.

In 1940, an astrologer by the name of Grant Levi read the horoscope of Hitler and foretold his self-destruction. "Hitler will kill himself," (p. 41, *Astrology for the Millions*); "that May, 1941 begins his decline (p. 54) and what he built . . . will scarcely outlive him by a single year" (p. 54). Continuing to Roosevelt, Levi predicted that ". . . he meets his Nemesis within eyeshot of being the first president to serve three terms, and . . . this is not his tragedy alone, but America's, and the world's also" (p. 80). All prophesies were printed and shelved before April, 1945. Roosevelt's third term ended in January, 1945; he died in April.

It is small matter that hundreds of astrologers predicted a different future for the Caesars, the Hitlers, and the Henrys of the world. Against the success of one, their failure counts little. Success is publicized, failure buried quietly; and people come to be convinced.

The Stars Control

The "stars" control a vast array of phenomena; as a functional alternative to science and religion, astrology helps people to order their lives in almost every dimension of life. For those who believe, the heavens will help them to know the time to plant and the time to harvest, the time to build and the time to break down, the time to speak and the time to keep silent, the time to love and the time to hate, for everything has its season given by the relation of the stars to the earth.

In Sumer and in Chaldea, people planted and gathered according to the monthly changes in the heavens. In Babylon and Assyria, war was planned and fought by the passage of the planets. From the time of the temple of Denderoh until today, people consult the stars in order to know what to do and when to do it. Business affairs, vacations, friendships, work, parties, travel, budgets and financial matters, diet, and style of life are but a part of behavior organized by the stars. The daily horoscope presented below was prepared by Jeanne Dixon for Saturday, the third of January, 1970 in *The Chicago Tribune.**

ARIES	(March 21–April 19): Boost your morale by putting on your finest attire. Get chores done quickly and concentrate on enjoying your contacts and relationships. Routine journeys turn out to be fun.
TAURUS	(April 20–May 20): New attachments hold much appeal. On all sides, Saturday should offer you peace and beauty. Go sightseeing or tour some favorite scenery.
GEMINI	(May 21–June 20): If you will get up and get started early, doing your full share cheerfully, everyone else tends to get into step with you. Plan a party for this evening.

(**Reprinted by courtesy of the Chicago Tribune.*)

CANCER (June 21–July 22): Take a cheerful approach to life Saturday. You'll attract others of like mood. Arrange a pleasure trip or plan some sort of festivity, according to the weather and your local climate.

LEO (July 23–Aug. 22): Take full advantage of the cooperative attitudes of people around you. Organize your hospitality so that all are shown your welcome. Social contacts made now promise to be of lasting satisfaction.

VIRGO (Aug. 23–Sept. 22): A brief journey may produce a bit of unplanned lunch. You have a better chance of meeting new and interesting people Saturday.

LIBRA (Sept. 23–Oct. 22): Use a bold, forthright approach, and go after what you want. There is a chance to add something long desired to your possessions.

SCORPIO (Oct. 23–Nov. 21): Take positive action to balance your budgets and obligations. Clear the way for some serious rearrangements coming up this spring. Seek entertainment, social activity this evening.

SAGITTARIUS (Nov. 22–Dec. 21): Keep your sense of humor going bright and strong. Your family may want to know the fine details of financial matters.

CAPRICORN (Dec. 22–Jan. 19): You can get the cooperation of a wide range of people for a new venture Saturday. Your diet will bear watching, as your appetite is quite active now. The lighter the leisure-time entertainment, the better.

AQUARIUS (Jan. 20–Feb. 18): Consider your position this morning; review your plans and economic progress carefully. Then put it all out of sight and mind for a personal holiday mood.

PISCES (Feb. 19–March 20): The initiative is in your hand Saturday; the sooner you do what you can with it, the better.

Millions of people read such horoscopes and believe them to be "their" horoscope. Still others pay part-time and full-time astrologers ten dollars and up for more precise information on how to organize their lives. Since there are more astrologers than sociologists, it would seem that astrology is more important to everyday life than sociology; yet we have no information on how many people organize how much of which portions of their lives by means of the art of astrology. Still less do we know the correlates of such behavior to class, religiosity, political affiliation, to demographic variables, or to aspirations. Astrology is an important social institution rather than fad, or fancy, and social research must begin to include key items in questionnaires in order to understand our social organization. At a minimum, each research design should include the items:

1. What is your sun sign?
2. Do you watch your horoscope?
3. Do you use your horoscope readings in:
   (a) business investments,
   (b) family,

(c) political issues,
(d) planning vacation,
(e) other?

Physical Phenomena and Metaphysical
The moon controls the tides and the sun the seasons of rain and snow. The Earth responds in subtle ways to the pull of the sun and planets. Mountains are born and chasms created by the convection currents of the Earth's magna which in turn respond to the gravitational effects of the moon. Fish spawn and insects follow the call of the months. The physical functions of the body are not immune to the turning of the Earth in orbit and the seas in tide. The alternation of day and night knows no source but the journey of the Earth around the sun.

If the biological phenomena of crops and animal life related to the wheeling of the stars is not enough to convince the intellectual, removed as he is from mundane interests, there is the wedding of astrology and mathematics to puzzle one—equally as convincing as the intimate relationship between geometry and geography as to the role of metaphysical constructs in shaping of empirical events. Just as the normal curve of the statistician finds expression in the data of human behavior, so too do the sun signs find expression in human behavior for the astrologer: who then is the metaphysician?

ENCOUNTER GROUPS AND SENSITIVITY GROUPS

Encounter groups must be recognized as an effective source of self for growing numbers of persons. These groups are based upon the existential phenomenological approach to experience exemplified in the work of Fromm (1955), May (1961), Allport (1961), Rogers (1961), and Maslow (1962) in conjunction with the pioneer efforts of those who organize T-groups, sensitivity training groups, encounter groups, marathon groups as well as less well-identified forms of encounter such as trips, festivals and retreats. When one examines the purposes and patterns in encounter groups, it becomes clear that the apparatus identified by symbolic interactional theorists about how self arises is to be found in these groups. Encounter groups then became functional equivalents to the primary groups of family, kin, and peers discussed by Mead and others as crucial to the generation of self.

In the first instance, the *focus is upon the self* as a quite specific subject of attention rather than upon products (in the market), entertainment (in mass communication and mass sport), and upon subject matter (in Establishment University). For the self to be the center of social discourse fulfills the first condition of socialization. This focus upon self was assumed by early symbolic interactions to be taken for granted in all social activity. Looking at the aims of encounter groups (as a generic term) these include developing personal understanding, accuracy in self-sensitivity, changes in life values as well as in overt behavior, responsibility for one's own fate, focus upon potentials rather than upon existing shortcomings, self-acceptance, self-healing, circumvention of defenses, self-disclosure, formulation of one's problems by one's self, review of personal experience in family, work, school, and military; in sum, the encounter demands a shared examination of self-image.

But also important to the generation of self is feedback from others—accurate, reliable, continuing, and relevant feedback. This the individual receives in plentiful and painful supply in the encounter group. Focus on self, feedback from significant others, together with resources for components out of which to construct self: values, attitudes, style, purpose, role (in the larger sense), requires one to view encounter groups as a new important source of self.

The raw material of self may be found in the subject matter brought into the groups. The following inventory comes from Weigel (1968) and can be seen to proffer to the individual options for *self* self-development.* The topics discussed in the order they occurred were:

1. open vs. closed minds: absolute values
2. the students' role in campus government
3. faculty involvement with students
4. freedom of choice of outside campus speakers (e.g., Nazis)
5. OSU as a conservative community, and its relation to the real world
6. matching individual student characteristics with those of different universities: value changes in college
7. when am I my brother's keeper?
8. drugs
9. stereotyping (e.g., hippies)
10. segregation
11. sex and homosexuality
12. sex and pregnancy: students' expectations of parents' reactions
13. confusion of goals for students, and responsibility to parents
14. the double standard of values for self and others
15. responsibility for one's own actions: determinism vs. free will
16. dogs and cats as beings with feelings
17. the courage to be imperfect

(*Reprinted with permission of R. G. Weigel, *marathon group therapy and marathon group discussion. A paper presented at the American Personnel and Guidance Association, Las Vegas*, 1968.)

18. effects of weather on human behavior
19. suicide
20. incest
21. self-diagnosis of mental disorders (medical students' disease)
22. the meaning of over-involvement in community service
23. how one forms relationships; characteristics of a friend
24. the Catholic Church and modern life
25. what religion has to offer to the modern student
26. alcohol
27. sex and the new morality
28. the affluent society and its problems for individuals
29. trial marriage
30. prostitution
31. abortion
32. birth control pills
33. the acceptance of medication or therapy as "weakness"
34. treatment facilities at OSU
35. vocational tests and counseling
36. how much one should allow those around him to influence him
37. friendship and jealousy
38. being concerned about how an individual feels without agreeing with his ideas
39. the draft and conscientious objectors
40. obligations to support national policy
41. survival in nuclear war
42. gun laws
43. typical female sexual feelings and behaviors
44. the worth of marathon group discussion

Encounter groups are being used also to repair self as well as to form it in the first instance. Bach (1966, 1967); Stoller (1967a, 1967b); Weigel (1968); Mintz (1967); Hurst and Uhlemann (1967); Fenner (1968) and others are pioneering in the use of encounter groups, especially marathon groups in psychotherapy.

Weigel has found that marathon encounter groups do have therapeutic efficacy:

With Groups A, B and C pooled, sign tests indicated that eleven of the thirty scales changed significantly in the predicted direction. Subjects in marathon treatment answered with fewer responses indicative of defensiveness (K decreased), hypochondrical concerns (Hs decreased), depression (D decreased), rebellion or nonconformity (Pd decreased), or dependency (Dy decreased). They answered with more responses indicative of constructive integration or ego strength (Es increased) and dominance (Do increased). These results would appear to reflect a parallel effect occurring in each of the three groups (p. 116).

There may be doubt about the long-range future of encounter groups; however I do not believe them to be a fad. The proliferation of these groups with their focus on self in the past few years requires that the social psychologist think through their meaning beyond their immediate purposes. We think the best way to understand encounter groups from the point of view of the sociologist is to see them as providing a new source for the private construction of self as social organization in complex systems becomes more and more within the purview of the business systems designer who, perforce, must discard self-structure as a primary source of social structure.

THE HIGHER LEARNING

Perhaps the most noteworthy factor to observe when comparing the differences in courses offered between Free and Establishment Universities is the difference in the objectives of the courses. As they relate to the development of the self, in general, the Free University courses provide one with the skills, understandings, and components with which to build an adequate and acceptable (to one's self) self-system. The major thrust of the Establishment University is to generate social systems and, secondarily, to generate a self-system which meets the minimal requirement for performance in large-scale establishments: school, work, polity, market, welfare, war, mass media, and so on. For every expert in designing the self-system, Establishment University produces a thousand experts to design and construct market systems, industrial systems, accounting systems, housing, transportation and communications systems, weapons systems, and agricultural systems. The principles of cybernetics are also applied to cities, to watershed areas, to pace technologies, and many others. What Establishment University does, it does well and will do better. All this does not cover up what it is not geared to do nor should it be taken as an apology for that which Establishment University does and should not be doing; ROTC, alienation of students, mass classes, and more.

The encounter courses offered in Free University stand in marked contrast to the courses in social work, education, sociology, psychology, and the rest offered by Establishment University. This is not to put down the courses in Establishment University, only to point out the differential consequences for generation of an adequate and satisfying self. Perhaps a point to be taken less lightly is the frequency of courses in Establishment University, especially in psychology, offering to train functionaries in LSOs the finer arts of molding, guiding, manipulating, motivating, and evaluating people in terms and in ways advantageous to the establishment, rather than in ways to constrain the establishment people. In particular, one could teach a course in consumer psychology to aid the consumer avoid the end runs around his ego to the depths of his unconscious rather than produce the Freudian revisionists of whom Marcuse speaks. At the present, these courses are taught to advertising types to help them use mass media to link private drives to business goals.

One cannot compare every course offered in Free University with its establishment counterpart. For one thing, most Free University courses are encounter courses while most courses in Establishment University are technique courses. Below is a comparison which, though not exhaustive of either organization, still permits one to see the major differences between the two with fair accuracy.

ART

Zombie Drawing
If you bring penpoints and microscopic eyes we can draw little itsy bitsy diddly-fuck things, cancel out what is artsy-fartsy, talk about Guys We Like (Names!).*

> AR 115, Drawing I M.W.F. 3(0–6)
> Freehand drawing covering selection of subject, proportion, perspective, line, texture, value, and composition. Media include pencil, conte crayon, charcoal, and ink.

MUSIC

Old Time String Band
This is a sometimes vain attempt to gather together for occasional evenings of pickin' and singin' in the old String Band Style. Meets sporadically, on the whim of whoever offers a location for us to meet.

> MU 152, Stringed Instrument Class S. 3(3–0)
> The playing of stringed instruments in the hands of students, emphasizing problems of public school music instruction.

EDUCATION

The Free University is a Purple Banana
An entirely unofficial (if you can get any less official) course spawned by a Coordinating Committee meeting at which there was much discussion of what the Free University is, used to be, ought to be, will surely be if you guys don't get your heads straight, etc. My humble home is yours for unhurried discussion, at length in a congenial (nonvoting) atmosphere, of the Free University, education community, and anything else. People of all levels of experience and involvement, i.e. you, are invited and welcome.

> ED 572, Social Foundation of Education. SS. 3(3–0)
> Examination of the social objectives and philosophy of education in relation to educational practices, and implications from a study of sociological data.

---

*These courses come from the Mid-peninsula Free University in California. The Free University course is given at the margin and its Establishment University counterpart is indented.

ENGINEERING

Cybernetics and the Disconnected Society

A one session seminar on our disconnected society and how models and technologies from cybernetics might be used to establish connection between individuals ethical ideals and the alternatives offered him by our social institution. The major models and technologies of cybernetics will be reviewed. Then the disconnected society will be examined in respect to the breakdown of connection between the ethical ideals of the major religious faiths and the decision processes of industrial society. Then a procedure will be explained how cybernetics might be used to connect religious, existential, and communist perspectives.

EG 102, Engineering Principles II, W. 3(2–3)
Prerequisite: EG 101
Analysis and solution of elementary engineering problems, including use of digital computers and basic graphics.

SOCIOLOGY

Fight Training for Couples

In our culture hostility and negative feelings are usually associated with the degeneration of a relationship. We have just learned to accept that, at times, partners in an intimate relationship do feel other than beautiful feelings towards each other. We have learned how to fight a fair fight with a loved one so that both can win. Try to read *The Intimate Enemy* by George Bach and Peter Wyden. Class limited to first 8 couples.

S 340, The Family, F. W. S. 3(3–0)
Prerequisite: S 100
The roles of the husband, wife, and children in the family, in the community and the coordination of family living with the school, church, and other community institutions.

PSYCHOLOGY

L'allegro

"Untwisting all the Chains that tie the Hidden Soul of Harmony."

In this group we will try to achieve Harmony in ourselves, and with others, emphasizing warmth and happiness. So that we can develop a deep involvement with each other the group will be balanced, limited in number, and closed to new members after the second meeting.

PY 415, Social Psychology, F. W. S. SS. 3(3–0)
Prerequisites: PY 100, S 100
Psychological bases of group behavior, including individual and group social adjustments.

SOCIAL WORK

Agnew Musicale

Do you get uptight around old people, young people, sick people, mentally ill? Then this course is not for you. Experience the mentally ill as REAL PEOPLE. You may find Agnew a challenge to your ability to communicate. Every Thursday the class convenes for a musical encounter with the patients in one of the wards. Oral and musical skills will be sharpened.

You will meet some turned on people. Discussion of the encounter experience follows at my home. Musical ability helpful. Empathetic nature a requirement.

> S 380, Introduction to Social Work, F. 5(5–0)
> Prerequisites: S 280 and S 281, or junior or senior standing.
> Purposes, setting, and activities types or social work. Philosophy principles, and problems. Principles of interviewing.

In a society where rationality has created a fabric much too flimsy from which to build a self-system, however stable and adequate from other perspectives, the Free University, as a genre, is most important to the human condition. In terms of the experiments in the underground church, the Free University, communes, and encounter groups, I believe that California should be given credit for its experimental searches into new sources of self for the entire country. I would like to present a few more of the course titles in that they further exemplify the difference in orientation between Free University and Establishment University.

> Trust, Touch, and Tenderness
> For Both to Win
> The Beautiful You Emerging
> Beginning
> Discovery of the Inner You
> Gentleness Encounter
> A Spring Thing
> The Free Woman
> Let's Go
> Men's Night Off
> Mountain Goat
> Sensual Contact
> Love
> Excitement and Growth in the Human Personality
> Nonverbal Encounter
> Vibrations
> Me, Again
> Astrology and You
> Is Your Guy Gay?
> Boffing: Super-High Love Trip
> Jungian Astrology
> *I Ching*
> Explorations in Psychedelics
> Country Karma
> To Be More Whole
> The Meaning of Death: Psychodrama Marathon
> Growth Marathon
> Consciousness in the Flesh
> The Relevance of Sade
> Sitting

Is the Future Inevitable?
Inner Growth Through Metaphysics and Meditation
Visionary Convocation for Sages, Madmen, Explorers, Teachers, Preachers, Tinkers,
Listeners, and General Folk.

And the relevance of course content for self-structure focus found in Free
University courses simply is not germane to the more social uses of course
content found in Establishment University:

AFROTC	Aerospace Studies
Ag	Agriculture Marketing
Ag Eng	Machinery and Hydraulic Systems Design
	Flow in Porous Materials
Agr	Crop Seed Purity
	Forest and Range Soils
Anat	Neurology
	Anatomy of the Horse
	Ultrastructural Cytology
An Sci	Essentials of Meats
	Wool Studies
Anthr	Cultural Ecology
	Comparative Social Structure
AROTC	Individual Weapons of the Army
	Principles of War
Art	Design I
	Interior Design
Atmos Sci	Introduction to Weather and Climate
	Theoretical Meteorology
Biochem	Intermediary Biochemistry
	Protein Biochemistry
Bio Sci	Cell Biology
	Principles of Animal Biology
Bot	Poisonous Plants
	Fungi and Human Affairs
Bus	Real Estate Law
	Management
Bus Acct	Income Tax
	Cost Analysis
Bus Fin	Credit Management
	Investment Policy
Bus Mar	Salesmanship
	Market Analysis
Bus Off	Typewriting
	Secretarial Machines
Bus Per	Personnel Management
	Collective Bargaining
Bus Prod	Industrial Procurement
	R & D in Industry

Bus Voc	Computer Programming
	Business Systems Development
Chem	Natural Science
	Glass Blowing
Div Eng	Surveying
	Soils Engineering
Econ	Money and Banking
	International Trade Theory
Educ	Introduction to Teaching
	Guidance in the Schools
Elect Engr	Linear Systems
	Random Signals

The sampling of the courses offered at Establishment University gives the reader a sense of the degree to which a contemporary public university is designed to service social systems rather than self-systems. These courses are vital to their purpose and their purpose is vital to everyone. These courses are highly sophisticated, jam-packed with useful knowledge, quite stimulating to both professor and student, and most valuable to the society. One must not lose sight of this while pondering the question of the relationship between self-system and the educational system in the course content of the Establishment University. Still less would we hold that these courses should be dropped and those of the Free University offered instead. Rather, it is certain that both kinds of curricula are vital to our emerging organization of education. Large-scale organizations are just too vital to be eliminated or crippled by derationalizing. Self-systems are just too important to be left to large-scale organizations to cripple and to erode.

There are two major developments in higher education which may ameliorate the situation to some extent. First there is the politicization of students on campus. Among their political concerns is the reversal of campus priorities. At present, for most faculty in large colleges and universities, the ranking of priorities places excellence of teaching last after publishing and service to the community. Service to the community is the euphemism used to refer to consultancies, grantsmanship, funded research, safe political activity, and testifying at congressional hearings.

After the CIA could no longer find political use for the National Student Association abroad, the NSA helped students at many major universities to get organized and to develop a platform. After Mario Savio and the Free Speech Movement at Berkeley, many irreversible changes occurred in student bodies across the nation. Significant to our interests here is the developing determination on the part of student political parties, especially the United Action Party, to reverse faculty priorities and force teaching excellence to become the major concern of professors. The situation has deteriorated to a point where, at universities such as the University of Colorado, thirty-four percent of the undergraduate classes are staffed by graduate students. Up to seventy-seven percent of the undergraduate teaching there involves graduate students in some capacity. For many professors, it is *déclasseé* to teach freshmen and sophomores.

Student leaders have identified the issues and are developing the political tools to reverse this set of priorities. If this movement succeeds and is joined with another, that which Easton (1969) refers to as the *Post-Behavioral Revolution*, then students just might humanize the university. After all, before businessmen, politicians, and the military discovered how useful academicians could be, the product of the university was "demi-urge," that half-man, half-god, the Renaissance man.

A word about the *post-behavioral revolution* is necessary. One should understand that the brief treatment given here does not reflect my opinion of the magnitude of its importance. In brief, Easton means to identify and support an educational revolution just beginning to be felt in the professions and on the campuses. Its essence is relevance and action directed toward the social and political crises of our time. The tenets of the movement are taken from Easton's presidential address to the American Political Science Association.

1. Substance must precede technique. If one must be sacrificed for the other—and this need not always be so—it is more important to be relevant and meaningful for contemporary urgent social problems than to be sophisticated in the tools of investigation. For the aphorism of science that it is better to be wrong than vague, post behavioralism would substitute a new dictum, that it is better to be vague than nonrelevantly precise.

2. Behavioral science conceals an ideology of *empirical conservatism*. To confine oneself exclusively to the description and analysis of facts is to hamper the understanding of these same facts in their broadest context. As a result, empirical political science must lend its support to the maintenance of the very factual conditions it explores. It unwittingly surveys an ideology of social conservatism tempered by modest incremental change.

3. Behavioral research must lose touch with reality. The heart of behavioral inquiry is abstraction and analysis and this serves to conceal the brute realities of politics. The task of post-behavioralism is to break the barriers of silence that behavioral language necessarily has created and to help political science reach out to the real needs of mankind in a time of crisis.

4. Research about and constructive development of values are inextinguishable parts of the study of politics. Science cannot be and never has been evaluatively neutral despite protestations to the contrary. Hence to understand the limits of our knowledge we need to be aware of the value premises on which it stands and the alternatives for which this knowledge could be used.

5. Members of a learned discipline bear the responsibilities of all intellectuals. The intellectuals' historical role has been and must be to protect the humane values of civilization. This is their unique task and obligation. Without this they become mere technicians, mechanics for tinkering with society. They thereby abandon the special privileges they have come to claim for themselves in academia, such as freedom of inquiry and a quasi-extraterritorial protection from the onslaughts of society.

6. To know is to bear the responsibility for acting and to act is to engage in reshaping society. The intellectual as scientist bears the special obligation to put his knowledge to work. Contemplative science was a product of the nineteenth century when a broader moral agreement was shared. Action science of necessity reflects the contemporary conflict in society over ideals and this must permeate and color the whole research enterprise itself.

7. If the intellectual has the obligation to implement his knowledge, those organizations composed of intellectuals—the professional associations—and the universities themselves cannot stand apart from the struggles of the day. Politicization of the professions is inescapable as well as desirable.

Such a set of tenets reorients academia drastically. From its present position of handmaiden to the business, financial, military, and industrial, agricultural interests, higher education moves to the human interests of the larger population. Add together the reappraisals and reorientations of the APSA, the American Sociological Association, the Sociology Liberation Movement, the Modern Language Association, and the American Historical Association, and one has a more human and less societal use of education. All is quiet in respect to psychology and economics, but even philosophy is under attack from the forces of liberation.

The net effect of the two movements described above may force the university to adopt a more balanced set of offerings—a set relevant to that revolution of hope demanded by Fromm. Such a university would be a better place for people and would find a better place in history.

MASS COMMUNICATION

A major difference between *neo-Gemeinschaft* and *Gemeinschaft* cultures is the emphasis placed on research and competence in the use and expansion of technology. *Gemeinschaft* communities view research as blasphemy. *Neo-Gemeinschaft*, like its parent society, is involved in on-going research and innovation. The freak community specializes in certain areas: art, music, and drugs which produce unusual or extraordinary states of consciousness.

The freak community's major use of technology in areas other than bio-chemistry and architecture (an example of which is the geodesic dome) is its use of the mass media. The freak community uses the mass media, especially the long-playing record and radio, for maintenance of communication, for maintenance of a shared cognitive map, for socialization, and for proselytization. Through their music, this culture presents its major value and belief systems and delivers its attacks on the surrounding culture of straight America.

In terms of the individual's self-structure, it is interesting to note that McLuhan (1964) makes a distinction between hot medium and cool medium, hot medium being that which extends a single sense in "high definition." High definition is a state of being well filled with data. Cool medium is that which provides low amounts of information but involves several senses (low definition). "Hot media are, therefore, low in participation, and cool media are high in participation or completion by the audience" (p. 36). The phonograph is a cool medium providing a high level of participation and, more important, providing a structural support for the production of self. A great deal of the socialization is accomplished through the long-playing record.

As noted in the section on the freak community, LP records and youth-oriented radio provides a continuing flow of ingredients readily adoptable as part of one's personal self-system. The lyrics below give one some idea of how LPs provide specific prescriptions for behavior as well as generalized directions for orientation of life:

"Mobius Trip"*
Collier
Prestige Music
H. P. Lovecraft II
H. P. Lovecraft

Walkin' down the street I feel like crashin'
Everybody's groovy all their eyes are flashin'
Do you think that this could be the time
To view the world behind a better mind
When everybody's really feelin' fine
A thought like that would really blow my mind.

In the park the air is cleaner
And the smell of grass is greener
Do you think that this could be the place
To view the world where only time's arrayed
It happened just like everybody said
You crossed the line and never left your head.

(*Reprinted with permission of H. P. Lovecraft Records for Phillips Records, c/o Mercury Record Corp., 35 E. Wacker Drive, Chicago 1, Illinois.)

" Brave New World"*
Steve Miller
ASCAP
Brave New World
The Steve Miller Band

We're traveling fast from the dream of the past
To the brave new world
Where nothing will last that comes from the past
It's a brave new world
Put a smile on your face as we walk through space
See the brave new world
Now as you begin you're born once again with a rising sound.

Chorus
Something new, nothing old, something true, something bold.

No spirit of the past can hold you back
From the brave new world
The direction to start is inside your heart
To the brave new world
If you're free in your heart you can make a new start
It's a brave new world
There's nothing to hide leave your troubles behind
It's a brave new world
I told you my friend and I'll tell you again your trip is begun.

Chorus
The direction to start is inside your heart
To the brave new world.

Ernest van den Haag (1957) has said, correctly, that the audience of mass media has come to expect to be sold something: goods, stereotypes, recipes for living. Van den Haag having said that, one expects that the mass audience will begin to pick and choose: to select rather than be sold. An adequate technology has the promise of returning art to mass communcation. If that happens, and I think it will, then the content of mass communication can be perceived on its own terms, without predigestion, without adulteration, bowdlerizing, and without explaining how a thing should be understood or appreciated. There it is: take it and make of it what you can and what you will. There is a mass media for pornography which didn't exist in forms available to all until recently. There are journals on radical politics, sociology, and education. There are publications for homosexuals, wife-swapping, swinging, drug use, *et cetera, et cetera, et cetera.* Van den Haag's observations were valid enough in 1957 but 1970 sees more frankness and freshness—for

(*Copyright © "Brave New World" by Steve Miller, Sailor Music (ASCAP).)

weal or for woe, mass communication is, as they say, beginning to let it all hang out.

That mass communcation remains a monstrous instrument for the managing and manipulation of people cannot be denied. In the short period between Eisenhower and Nixon, mass communication has evolved from the making of presidents to the selling of them. That advertising uses sexuality for commercial purposes while conventional legal institutions deny it to human use is only too true. That the programming of TV divorces people from power and politics, but makes them "happy," justifiably is condemned. All this being true, I still want to emphasize the potential of mass communication for servicing the self.

RETIREMENT COMMUNITIES*

Most of the attention in this section has been given over to the new sources of self for those at the young adult end of the population pyramid. At the other end, more and more people are being separated from society with little structural support remaining for the social identities which they have come to believe they are. Cumming & Henry (1961) have examined carefully the problems created by separating social self from its social anchorages. For many retirees this does approach tragedy.

But many other persons find sufficient anchorages in a variety of "manufactured occasions" to sustain self in a most satisfying way. In one retirement center, Tucson Estates, several of a wide variety of manufactured occasions permit the individual to choose how he shall organize his behavior. It is important to note that the self emerges partly out of the schedule of manufactured occasions and partly out of the exercise of options on the part of the person concerned.

Among the options are the occasions manufactured within the retirement communities—games, dances, shows, meetings, visits, teas, sports, parties, and so on. Some occasions are manufactured by those affluent enough to provide the accouterments. There are a number of occasions which link the retired to structures in the community as well; sometimes a church is in need of a part-time organist; one school permits a retired person to assist in the shop program which is an enormously satisfying and socially valued source of self for this man.

Close to Tucson Estates is "Old Tucson," now a TV production set. The casting is spread out among "old-timers." Several of the men and women organize their lives on the chance that they will get a bit part in a TV western.

---

*I am indebted to Edward Knop for his helpful discussion and ideas here.

One such bit part goes a long way in providing satisfaction in self. One writes to dozens of friends and relatives across the country telling them to watch for the program in which one appears, and then one waits a few months for another bit part.

Retirement communities are more than storage bins for the discards of military, industrial, financial and commercial LSOs; given an adequate retirement income, some people can participate in enough of these manufactured occasions to survive as a social-psychological unit of organization and operation.

CHAPTER 7

Private Uses of Self

Homo sum, Nil humani a alienum puto
... Terence

As Goffman (1963) stresses, much of our definition of mental ill health relies upon comparisons of actual behavior to situational norms. If a person fails to stay uptight to the sociology of it all, the general diagnosis is that he is lacking in some crucial dimension of human competence. And if he doesn't stay uptight, the obligation is to shield the delict and, hence, sustain the legitimate definition of the situation.

But to order one's behavior in ways compatible with large-scale enterprises is to be passive, bored, unfeeling, and one-sidedly cerebral, as Fromm (1968) points out. And, as he also says, technological society must be humanized. In *The Revolution of Hope*, Fromm speaks of humanistic planning, humanistic management, humanized consumption, and psychospiritual renewal as necessary to the reordering of modern society. There can be no dispute with this thinking. However, as crucial as are Fromm's suggestions, they are not sufficient. The arguments presented in Chapter 5 on the rational version of society-without-self hold. Large-scale business, religion, education, industry simply do not (nor should they) focus upon the self-system as a unitary whole. However humanistic the goals of large-scale enterprise, the rational means to pursue those goals must include specialization, computers, mass production, and all of the technology of modern business. In a humanized complex *Gesellschaft*, there is still no place for a humanized self to arise and a humanized self is what is lacking for the masses in modern society. The developments in contemporary society repair the damage done to the human spirit to some extent. The Free university, the Zodiac, the underground church and such provide a media in which self can arise and flourish. We considered the new sources of self in the previous chapter. It is necessary to think about private uses of self in this chapter in both theory and practice.

As one reads through the material in the next sections, it is important to understand that the most human uses of self are now defined as corrupt when employed for private purposes. But most of these uses are not corrupt in and of themselves. Sexual activity of all sorts, use of psychedelic aids, pleasureful and painful experience are regularly used in societies to solve organizational problems of motivation, dedication, discipline, and solidarity. The most general rule one can abstract is that such activity is "moral" when put to social ends and "corrupt" when not used in social arenas. Thus, drinking alcohol is defined as "alcoholism" and a disease entity only when used privately to excess. Using alcohol to excess in male solidarities is not only not defined as a "problem" but, rather, the goal-state to achieve. The physiological and psychological harm of religious fervour is only condemned when it interferes with "role performance."

Most pleasureful and painful activities continue to be monopolized to social purposes even though those social purposes are presently satisfied by other means. In the past, monopoly of the most lively ways in which one could be human meant that one could be human only by being coterminous with the social order. In the future, one will be able to be human only by putting to private use the charming, challenging, engrossing, enlivening activities historically monopolized by society.

The role of camp in this area should not be underestimated. Camp functions to end that monopoly item by item. If camp does anything of social significance, it neutralizes the *moral* content defined into the symbols associated with prescribed and proscribed pursuits. Many young people are able to "enjoy" themselves in private ways as a result of the past successes of camp. Most of us are more comfortable with private use of self in such pursuits after such has been thoroughly camped. Some of us are so uptight that we can enjoy such commodities as sex, danger, drugs, pornography, and pain only if disembodied and prepackaged. Much of what we call "the rackets" package such commodities as gambling, sex, and sin in order to mass-merchandise them for us. And some of us are so "moral" that we can seek self-gratification and fulfillment only in the interstices of mass society. We use devious ways to experience pain and danger, pleasure and joy— through our children, our cars, our credit cards, and our wars. However else we use these means, some of us use them to the same end as do others use the rackets: to surreptitiously test and express our human condition: it is better than nothing, but still not a viable human condition.

CORRUPTION: THEORY

Social Uses of Psychogenics

In a mechanically consolidated society (Durkheim, 1964), particularly strong devices are required to bind together the units of organization which, in their similitude, would otherwise compete one with another, or, in any case, since such units are alike in structure and function, there is only episodic need to support one another. In organically consolidated societies, units within are continuously dependent upon each other for the supplies requisite to survival: the same strong devices binding *Gemeinschaft* components are not required for social purposes and *may* be put to private uses. The more rationally management attends to the details of organization, the less need is there for binding devices deriving from the psychological and social-psychological capacities of individuals and congeries of individuals to be utilized for these social purposes.

For example, if a given organization is to remain solvent, it must generate and maintain a line of meaning with information flow in which the principles of accounting are followed closely. In an organization possessing only limited technology in this area, there must be complex teams of persons organizing their capacities in extensively constrained ways in order to generate that line of meaning: accounting. With the introduction of computer technology, dozens and dozens of little old ladies and little old men no longer need use their psychobiological capacity to generate that particular line of meaning. That line of meaning can be programmed into the computer. An electromagnetic state of a machine replaces a psychological state of many persons. A rational organization no longer needs ranks of people trained to believe they *are* accountants and, in addition, the psychological capacities of these persons may (a) be turned to other social uses, (b) be used for private purposes, or (c) atrophy.

Another case in point is even more revealing: a religious service may be "primitive" or "modern." If it is modern, the definition of the situation will be generated more from the architecture of the building than from the emotional states of the participants. In affluent societies, grand cathedrals, magnificent stained-glass windows, powerful organs, rich tapestry, impressive choirs, professionally trained clerics, and tightly organized services reduce the need for persons to invest themselves and their psychobiological capacities to generate a given line of meaning called "the religious service."

A store-front church or a "primitive" community does not have access to these nonpsychological structural supports for the generation of meaning. Participants must invest themselves as selves in total sorts of ways. In such services, religious fervor is generated and permits differentiation of this occasion from all others. In the course of achieving the definition of the situation desired, participants turn on, and are turned on, to specific psychological states: awe, piety, joy, humility, reverence, fervor in various combinations. In so doing, extraordinary psychological states are, in fact, achieved. When the states are manifest in face, in behavior, in ecstasy, then there can be no doubt about which definition of the situation holds. What is achieved in modern service by architecture, accouterments, and specialists is achieved in "simpler" societies by use of one's human capacities. There *is* more spirit in the services of poorer churches. In order for the line of meaning to emerge and to be sustained, poor churches must depend on psychological states.

Many societies use psychedelic aids in order to expediate the task of generating extraordinary psychological states. Alcohol, peyote, pain, eroticism, hunger, song, and fatigue have been used to facilitate extraspecial states. As the church "modernizes," such supports become less useful and may be turned to more private purposes. While such psychedelic adjuncts *are* being used by a society as a means to generate the psychological state in question, it is mandatory that *nonsocial* use of psychedelia be defined as corrupt. More generally, any time psychological states are used to bind people into social systems and psychedelic agents are used to speed people toward that state, then those states and those agents must be defined as "sacred" and appearance of either outside the occasion must be defined as corrupt.

The psychological state used to consolidate any given social system varies widely among different cultures as does the psychedelic agent used. Until the social system becomes "rational" it is necessary to tie people into the system and to use their psychobiological capacities. Society maintains its monopoly on the self and the psychedelic aid until other, more dependable ways of generating a line of meaning are invented and adopted.

It is the thesis of this section that large-scale establishments require neither the self nor *extra*-ordinary psychological states in order to bind in and bind off system from nonsystem. When this is true, self, psychological states, and psychogenic agents may then be used in private ways without defining such use as "corrupt." Sex, food, alcohol, drugs, danger, fervor, pain, pleasure, and fatigue continue to have social meaning to be sure, but the point to focus on is that the monopoly of self and psychological state required in *Gemeinschaft* becomes dysfunctional in advanced *Gesellschaft*. If a complex organization is to process masses of persons through the routines of its structure, it must do so as rationally as possible. In the concrete instance, this means stripping the excess baggage away and using as little of any given person as is necessary. This reduces to a signature and a check for thousands of social systems each involving millions of persons. It reduces to one or some few more units for still more rational systems. Colgate as a complex organization can survive if as many as a few million people do as little as pick up a tube or two of toothpaste a year.

It is too cumbersome for large-scale organizations to "waste" time generating emotional orientations when cognitive or behavioral orientations will suffice. And the generating of emotional states obstructs the disengagement routines at the portals of social space, so the modern organization sets up routines which eliminate all there is about a person except that which is minimally necessary. It is this context in which it is sensible to say that the separation of self and society is rational.

I do not regard it a tragedy that self is divorced from large-scale organizations. Given that large-scale organizations begin to serve human ends in place of the ends of corporate growth, then I would hold that it is well that the separation continue. I would hold that large-scale establishments are able to do many things well: among these is not the construction of self. As I have pointed out in the previous chapter, there are now sources of self apart from formal organizations. And, as painful as it might be to those of us who were socialized to match the social order, what was once defined as corrupt is now necessary to serve private ends rather than social. Some of the private uses of self and psychological states are presented in brief detail below.

The Protestant Ethic

It was, more than any other religious movement, Puritanism and Calvinism which tied self to social order with Divine sanction. The linking of men to specific occupational identities was, for Luther, a reflection of Divine will. Rather than a fate to enjoy, it was a fate to which to submit. But with Baxter in *Saints Everlasting Rest*, wealth and its acquisition in pursuit of one's calling reflected God's glory as much as His will. The psychological change in orientation is subtle, but crucial. What was once corruption became, under Protestantism, sacred. The real moral objection to wealth was relaxation in security of possession and yielding to the pleasures of the flesh. Asceticism became a standard part of self under puritanism. In Puritanism, hard, continuous labor was labor for the glory of God. The emphasis upon a clearly established calling or profession is, in the Puritan ethic, also a requisite for a state of grace. Add together asceticism, a calling, hard labor, and stewardship and seal it with divine sanction and God becomes a God of capital growth and productive use of capital.

The Epicurean Ethic

For those who are superfluous to the economic order and have unearned income of high and sustained order, the Protestant ethic is an awkward ethic. It is replaced by the Epicurean ethic which sanctions the *consumption* of wealth if done with elegance, taste, and expertise (Young, 1962). For those who are superfluous to the productive order and have income of low order, the means to the pursuit of the Epicurean ethic is severely constricted. However, it is not entirely alien to this condition. Soul music, soul food, and soul are the underclass counterparts to the Epicurean ethic as expressed by the leisure class.

As more and more young people find the means, they desert the Protestant ethic *en masse* in pursuit of the Epicurean ethic. The religious teachings of the old religion have little to say about either ethic, however the new commandments outlined above provide more support to the Epicurean ethic than the old commandments supported the Protestant ethic.

Camp

In a paper entitled *Camp and Corruption* (1968), I discussed the neutralizing function of camp. Sacred symbols and protected activities became archaic in the course of the evolution of society. When such symbols are outdated *and* continue to hold sacred meaning, they become obstacles to new forms and new orders. It is then functionally important that the sacared content be removed in order that people feel neither discomfort nor guilt in omission of the old, or commission of the new. Just as a person must be degraded in the adult socialization process in order to *resocialize* him, a symbol must be degraded in connection with its standing on the scale of sacredness. Camp does this excellently well. To camp on something is to have fun with it rather than to make fun of it. If it is neutralized, it then becomes the raw material for other occasions. In particular, religion becomes available for private use, as does creativity, meditation, clothing, pain, song, sex, self, words, poems, and anything else no longer required for the social ends of post-*Gesellschaft* society.

CORRUPTION: PRACTICE

Style

As consumption becomes a central focus, an Epicurean ethic displaces the Protestant ethic. The Epicurean ethic organizes behavior around *styles* of expression. The Epicurean ethic requires that whatever one does, it be done with style, elan, and dedication. As the self comes to be used for private purposes one is able to use modern technologies to taste, to view, to hear, to think, to perceive, to integrate—in a word, to be. This point is in contrast to the use of technology for business, entertainment or, say, military purposes. Some sense of this Epicurean expression of style is seen in what is termed "putting it together." Comportment, thing, garb, speech, and hair: lots of hair. When one thinks about the social order—age, class, sex, kin, and occupational differentiations—one observes that garb, hair, and comportment serve as stable cues to one's "place" in that order. As these differentiations become "irrational" to the purposes of organizations in advanced *Gesellschaft*, such items can be put to private uses without harm to the social order. Thus, as sex differentiations become a matter of unconcern to mass communication or mass market, hair and clothing can be used to express a given individual's "style." In a social order where sexual differentiations are crucial to support the division of labor, then cues to one's sex must be generated, made public, and inserted into the self-system so that people conceive of themselves as either men or women. Just as color or ethnicity, may or may not be used as a basis for the divisions of labor, so sex might or might not be so used. If it happens that sex is not used for generation of social order, then hair cues and movement patterns as well as clothing need have no particular sociosexual meaning. At that point it becomes unnecessary to define as corrupt the use of clothing, hair, and comportment for personal reasons. Charles Winick (1968) has provided us with an excellent treatment of the desexualization in American life. The sexual differentiation in our culture is losing its supports in furniture, clothing, story lines, color, opera, literary and political styles, perfumery and more. Winick's scholarship is surpassingly good in developing the evidence of this desexualization. Masculinity is going the way of the horse and buggy while business has been its executioner.

In "Camp and Corruption," I made the point that camp can be viewed as a social process by which sacred meaning is neutralized for cultural items, with the result that these items may be used differently without incurring the wrath of society. That which was once sacred no longer draws social animosity, after it has been "camped" upon for a while. It is interesting to note the targets of camp are the practices which were at earlier times sacred to the "natives." As stated in that paper, the concern of camp is to have fun with something rather than to condemn it or to celebrate it. After being the target of camp, almost anything could then be put to private use. The early targets of camp have included sex, in which masculinity is toyed about; art, in which mawkish sentiment is satirized; song, in which true love is depicted as juvenile; and patriotism, in which the war machine is a put-on. You can get most any of these at Alice's Restaurant.

Exploration

To explore the dimensions of the human experience is an adventure denied to most of us still locked tightly into the social order. There are many dimensions to explore: perception, creativity, imagination, eroticism, meditation, intimacy, and artistry. But inasmuch as these have been monopolized and used for social organizational purposes, the constraints produced thereby have severely limited our experience of our potential in these dimensions. Casteneda (1968) has spoken of the brain as a valve which shuts off experience. The reopening of that valve is the aim of thousands of determined young people who have read Casteneda and who understand also that experience no longer needs such tight constraints as perhaps was the case when society was less "well" organized.

The use of drugs still continues to be a commodity monopolized for social use from the point of legal establishment. However, physicians provide escape clauses for many people for many drugs, stimulants and tranquilizers in particular. Any drug with palpable physical impact can be used for "turning on" to nonsocial forms of experience. These facts, together with the fact that many of the social uses of drugs are obviously (to the seeker) of less than prime importance have generated serious questions concerning the continuation of that monopoly. For example, most students I know are aware of the extensive use of drugs in college and commercial athletics. Amphetamines, vasodilators, analgesics, male hormones, and anabolic steroids are commonly used in all sports activities. The drugs are administered by trainers, coaches, and student assistants who have little medical training and less legal authority. Most young people are intelligent enough to think through the double standards of drug use and understand the lack of standards for social use. The monopoly over drugs, alcohol, eroticism, and other psychedelics has been discarded by the establishment as it has turned to business schools for "rational" means to advance specific goals. These psychedelics then become available as private means to private goals. This is not to say that drugs are indispensable to perception, awareness, and mastery; but the fact is that drugs help achieve this, and that is reason enough for their use. In a most unusual book, Carlos Casteneda writes of the years he spent with Don Juan, a Brujo and Yanqui Indian from Sonora, Mexico, learning the uses of peyote, jimson weed, and other plants for opening the doors to perception and awareness. He narrates the cycles of peyote use and recounts his sensations of cold, thirst, and discomfort disappeared and, in their stead, how a sense of warmth and excitation overcame him. His voice took on new qualities and provided new meanings available only to him. A feeling of drowsiness gave way to extreme lucidity, and a bee loomed in his perceptual field with devastating and extraordinary clarity. He reported being able to see in the dark and to see *all* of the objects around him. The work continues with an analysis of the teachings of Don Juan.

This is neither to proselytize for the private use of drugs nor to condemn such practice, but to understand and to think through the use of drugs in generating self-systems and social systems. Perhaps the way this point can best be made is by referring again to Durkheim's notion of mechnical solidarity. In many folk societies, the males of the community are only marginally dependent on each other. The mechanical devices to bind males into a solidarity must be strong indeed. In many *Gemeinschaft* settings, male solidarities have a monopoly over alcohol (The Lunahauna), over marijuana (Mexico), or pornography (U.S., Japan, Western Europe) and so on. These monopolies bind otherwise hostile, semi-savage, or indifferent individuals into a valued relationship which, as occasion arises, can easily be turned to more constructive enterprise: building, planting, defending, comforting, feeding and such. As these tasks become institutionalized, the social utility of the male solidarity declines as does the utility of the monopoly assigned to that solidarity in respect to any given bonding device. Private uses become possible and such use ceases to be defined as corrupt.

Activism

Many persons in *neo-Gemeinschaft* will use their training, study, knowledge, skill, and shrewdness to shape and reshape the parameters of culture. In Shaugnessy's terms, these are the movers and shakers of the world forever it seems. At present, we see many people use their time and human capacities to reshape the uses and form of contemporary society. Two such kinds of activism seem to serve as more immediate challenges to those who would turn to more public uses of self. Even though such uses advance the interests of large numbers of people, it is still sensible to speak of this use of self as private in that the constraints on the form and shape of self are not imposed by the table of organization of large-scale enterprise.

Senator Gaylord Nelson has initiated a nation-wide teach-in on the question of environmental control and quality. Before the final chapter is written in that book, whole generations of young people will find meaning, purpose, direction, and use of their psychobiological capacities. To these generations will accrue self-esteem, self-image, self-involvement, self-development, and self-interest . . . all necessary to the emergence of a self. At Colorado State University, an Environment Corps has been established. They have been given a task by Ian McHarg (and others) which they have accepted gladly. He began the challenge by stating that ". . . The young people here are the first generations to have no future . . ." given the present course of society. He diagnosed the trouble as a "planetary disease" in which the pathogens are, among others, "Dow Chemical, the A.E.C., and the Pentagon." He asserted that "we must battle them tooth and nail if we are to save the human race." There is little doubt that this arena will serve many people as an arena in which to express the activism which, since it finds few establishment sponsors, must find private sponsors.

There is another, somewhat less important arena in which activists will find opportunity to go against the windmills of establishment. Ralph Nader is the leading protagonist of consumerism and a lot of people with time and talent will rally to his cause. This may be the form in which people invest themselves in the course of activism . . . or perhaps another form will arise. Whatever the case, the fact is that there are many causes which advance the ends of peace, dignity, equality, and humanity, and to which active and idealistic people may give of themselves. By so doing a self emerges and subsists.

Instrumental

A great many people are required to act as cadre for the LSOs as these serve the general goals of society or the special goals of organization. Many will be involved in holistic ways in which self and society will continue to be twinborn. Doctors, lawyers, merchants, chiefs; many will think that they are indeed these things. But some will know that they are more than a doctor, more than a minister, more than a professor, yet will find satisfaction in using their considerable talent to social ends. Precisely because other uses are possible, it becomes possible for this usage to be private.

There is little doubt that for many professionals, the social identities that are lodged in the social organization are long-takes and demand all of the skill, talent, and ingenuity of professionals. However, one should not overestimate the potential of large-scale organization for providing self-structure. Many professionals find that they must submit to a retooling process periodically if they are to remain useful to their employer. A recent TV documentary entitled "Graphic Communications: They Used to Call It Printing," makes the point that the technology of data gathering and dissemination is changing so rapidly that a person entering the field now can expect to change career lines at least four times during his lifetime.

To tie identity to such a social order is dangerous business. In the first place it is necessary to resocialize a person in addition to retraining in order to get him to believe he is something different. In the second place, it is necessary to do a good bit of damage to one's self-structure. In the course of trading new identities for old it is necessary to treat the old identity, heretofore cherished, as though it were less than adequate. Beyond this, many professional people find that they have duties which are far removed from what they think they are. For example, many psychiatrists, chemists, and historians are doing administrative and clerical tasks much to the harm of the self-structure. The idea of a psychiatrist without a patient is a nonsense notion. One needs the social-structural supports for any given professional identity and, in a changing milieu, those supports have an odd way of slipping from under one's self-structure.

There is another problem for professionals in locating their self as a holistic entity in the table of organization of particular institutions or particular fields. In a very provocative work, Bennis and Slater (1968) predict the emergence of "temporary society." While we cannot be certain of the direction of evolution to be taken by given societies or societies generally, the fact remains that Bennis and Slater made a good case for their vision. It remains for social psychologists to think through the implications of a temporary society for the generation of self. On the face of it, their position appears to lend support to mine—that new sources of self are necessary for most people in the future, and even perhaps for the "professional." The argument in Bennis and Slater is that if people are formed into task forces on a temporary basis to deal with non-recurrent problems, moving to non-recurrent jobs in non-recurrent organizations situated in non-recurrent locations and using non-recurrent bodies of knowledge, then it is difficult indeed to locate self in social order. As Bennis and Slater note (p. 79), feelings of alienation arise when an individual is deprived of a permanent reference group toward whom he feels a bond and who depend upon him for one or two points of specialization which define his role in that group. When tied to a continuing social base, some of the damage to self in terms of human diversions is repaired vicariously by role others through whom life can be experienced in manifold ways. But, Bennis and Slater continue, if the specialist is separated from this permanent reference group and left only to his own resources, he becomes less human. It does not follow that since many people find life challenging and satisfying as professionals we can depend upon the existing forms of professional role-performance to continue forever. If Bennis and Slater are correct, we may find that even professionals are not immune to alienation.

The Rackets

The kind of activity engaged in by the lonely people in Las Vegas and described by Thomas Wolfe in *TKKTFSLB** may occupy the remaining

---

The Kandy Kolored Tangerine Flake Streamlined Baby.

years for those of us who cannot make private use of our individuality or who cannot develop authentic counter cultures. Gambling, spectator sports, playboy packaged sex, commercial television, mobile home parks, souvenir shops, Greyhound bus tours, shopping at Sears and Roebuck, eating at Howard Johnson's, going to Paris, flying United, and becoming a master-charge freak are examples of the rackets that will service those who cannot service themselves.

The point common to people who resort to rackets as structural supports for organizing "free time" is that they are conditioned by involvement in mass society to be passive participants in mass produced and mass consumed sex, excitement, sin, and sport. The chief point contrasting those who depend upon prepackaged expressive activities from those who package their own sins is that the former are standardized and, for the latter, sin is handcrafted. But the product offered by the rackets requires little personal investment, and therein lies the fault. Many people are not capable of presiding over their own sins and enjoying them fully. Thus, they retreat to the safety of commodity sin rather than risk the creative potentials of private sin. I think we are seeing the last generation of people who were socialized to honor the societal monopoly over pleasureful things.

Still, there are thousands of dentists from Des Moines, salesmen from Detroit, and journeymen machinists from Dallas who are unable to yield to activities heretofore defined as corrupt. For these people, an ersatz life is all that is possible. As much as one feels horror at the sight of housewives finding existence only through shopping with master-charge or lonely old women enjoying themselves before slot machines in Las Vegas, the fact remains that this is better than nothingness.

I think it was the "fugs" who developed the best ideological arguments for "fugging." Their line of reasoning is that "to masturbate is human, to fuck, divine." Those of us socialized to honor the social monopoly over erotic symbols and sexual behavior can force ourselves to see an occasional skin flick or to buy a subscription to *Playboy*. Those who are less dependent on social order find that nothing so human is so alien. Perhaps the entire realm of pleasurable things will become, by being a *fait accompli* or camp, available for private use in the near future.

An Inventory

Listed are specific examples of ways in which people can use themselves—ways other than the advancement of goals of large-scale organizations. These items are taken from the December 19–24 issue of the *Berkeley Barb* and serve to illustrate a fraction of the private uses a person can make of his self-structure and human psychobiological capacities.

As a volunteer in the
Abortion Communications Center
Berkeley Health Information Center
Black Man's Free Clinic
Central Committee for Conscientious Objection
Citizens Alert
Contra Costa Suicide Prevention Answering Service
Drug Crisis Clinic
Free Church
G.I. Help
Heliotrope
Huckleberry's for Runaways
Music Switchboard
People's Office
Police Conduct Complaint Center
Sexual Freedom League
Switchboard
War Resister's League

And in still more private uses in
Pottery classes
Fine Arts classes
Film-making and Acting workshop
Jazz Interpretive Dancing
Truth Study Center
Fiction Writers' Workshop
Bible trip to Mardi Gras
Modern Sex Institute
Sensuality Seminar
Bay Area Swingers
Nudist Club
Encounter Group (Gay and Straight)

And, more private still, from the "People" ads:
MINNEAPOLIS COUPLE:
We are educated and sensitive.
We seek a warm, sincere girl.
P. O. Box 000, Minneapolis

BI hip young chick seeks same for
threesome. POB 0000, Sunnyvale
VERY ATTRACTIVE COUPLE
She 36-24-36 He 6′ 190 and
hung both early 30 We dig French
Greek movies photos and

uninhibited sex couples and
females phone photo
assures quick answer
P. O. Box 000, Concord

YOUNG man 30, attr. College grad.,
sensitive, intelligent and discreet
Seek quiet, warm female. Box
0000, S. F. 00000

INSTANT RELIEF to any woman
with a VIVID imagination. Personal visit optional. 000-0000

STUDS—DARE to be farout! Wow
male 23 gdlkg. wants to do your
thing. Send photo of your thing.
to POB 0000 S. F. 00000

SKIERS serious only bi guy 38
wants weekend buddy for no. shore
slopes. Apres action optional Box
0000 Menlo Park

PROFESSIONAL cauc. man, 38,
stable, cultured, not bad looking,
warm lover, seeks meaningful relationship with educated, attra., af-
fectionate woman who enjoys
sports, music, art, travel, and is
definitely not overweight. 000-
000 000 S. F. 00000

HANDSOME HUNG YOUNG MAN
SEEKS SAME. PO Box 0000 San Jose

FRENCHIE LIKES GIRLS to date
him. Girls call 000-0000

BROADS, ladies, girls, women,
wives, daughters, sisters, mothers,
Ray's in need of female companion-
ship. If you fit into any of the
above categories and have no weird
hangups phone him at 000-0000
Apt. 000

LEARN SELF-HYPNOSIS
Get into Orbit
Group classes and indiv. tutoring
Free brochure
School of Hypnosis
S. F. 000-0000

Lonely att man 40 wants liberal
girl for sex love or whatever comes
want to give and get me a little T.L.C.
for Xmas call Tom 000-0000 00
to 10:00 AM or 0 to 1:00 AM.

WOMAN, evolved, mature, likes
involvement w/ man who digs Asian
philos., relig., encounters Bx 0000
Dublin 00000   000-0000   4-8 pm

GAY grad., 28, wants to meet
cleancut/sincere guy 24-30.   Bill
000-0000 after 0:00 pm wknites

HANDSOME Bi Negro Male, 23,
seeks roommate to share modern
bachelor apt downtown SF 18-25
Must be student in music or employed, play piano, read music,
be quiet in nature.   Write Box 000
000

TOTAL INTRA-GROUP LOVE
plus group sex equals group marriage!
Ohio couple & SF man seek gal 18-40, no
swingers: 000-0000

GAY GIRLS FAMILY OF 3 GIRLS
NEEDS 4th for the 3rd.   Must be
under 30.   Hip responsible fem.
P. O. Box 00000 00000.

WELL BUILT GUY WISHES TO
meet girl who is hungry for a
man.   Couples also answered.   Meet
anywhere SF area.   Discreet.   PO Box
0000   Vellejo 00000

MALE WHITE 28 Prof. type would
like to meet same to age 40,
single or married, stocky build,
with nylon or satin fetish, San
Francisco area.   Sincere, strictest
confidence, discretion.   Reply C.S.

OUT OF TOWN businessman would
like to help young attractive girl
with expenses write this week to
Box 00, SF. 00000

EROTIC COUPLES-Swingers wkly
rendezvous -How-Where-When to swing.
000-0000

THINKING OF PLACING AN AD
IN THE BARB? Do it all by phone.
For details call HALFWAY (000)
000-0000, 7-7 PM, M-F.

PARTY PAD WANTED -very nice,
private & large. Van   000-0000.

EROTIC COUPLES-SWINGERS-
Wkly RENDEZVOUS/ how-where-
when to swing, 000-0000 Joy.

The interesting thing about the ads and notices appearing in the underground press is that they fully and frankly acknowledge the desirability of using eroticism, creativity, pain, skill, knowledge, as well as other psychobiological capacities in private ways. There are about 200 such underground papers and a handful of magazines—*Avant Garde, Evergreen,* and others—which implicitly communicate to their readers that private uses of abilities are neither wrong nor harmful.

In addition to the underground press, there is the beginnings of a movement to remove the onus of illegality from such practices. This movement takes many forms, ranging from efforts to legalize pot to efforts to change abortion laws. The central focus of this movement is summarized in the attempt to eliminate "crimes without victims." This idea is to eliminate from the statute books of the various plenary jurisdictions those acts presently defined as illegal but which have no "victim" other than the person(s) involved. Thus, smoking pot, birth control, varieties of sexual experience, gambling, pornography, alcohol, vagrancy, would not be against the law. All the harmful second and third-order consequences which derive only from the fact of illegality would be spared those who cannot find human meaning within the limits of behavior now permitted.

The consequences of this happening, termination of the monopoly of society over the supplies of pleasure, should not be left unexamined. The number of people available to fight wars, take graduate study, accumulate capital, participate in resolving social issues, mow lawns, collect garbage, attend football games, buy now and pay later, and raise families might decrease. For a society to be unable to staff a war machine is no great loss to history, nor is a sharp reduction in child-producing families a loss. Both may well be so advantageous that other consequences become secondary. But the loss of people to define issues and identify interests for all sectors of the population is not a matter to take lightly. On balance, I think we have more to gain from the elimination of the practice of defining things as corrupt than from continuation of the practice. The payoff in self and in the experience of self in palpable ways is of overweening importance.

THE POLITICS OF EXPERIENCE: R. D. LAING

One must agree with Laing (1967) that one exists only as one experiences himself as the center of experience and experiences himself as the center of behavior. The modalities of such experience are lost to one in mass society composed of large-scale establishments as the typical media for experience. This is the point of Chapter 5.

Involvement in such media produces a "shriveled, desiccated" human fragment and one must, in order to be human, tear asunder the "veils of mystification" and undergo an intensive unlearning in order to be able to experience the world afresh: with innocence, truth, and love. Such are the teachings of R. D. Laing and they are truly important. Marcuse (1964) offers "The Great Refusal" as prologue to being human. Laing goes beyond this to prescribe the politics of experience as the central step in becoming human.

To undo the terrible harm done to our capacity to be, requires that we insist on the right to experience and be experienced. It means to reject as a model of self that "normality" which is the product of repression, denial, projection, sublimation. It means the rejection of *any* modality of experience which has shriveled us and which requires we take as models of sanity those who act and experience life in short, superficial, and one sidedly cerebral ways. "Sane" men, as Laing observes, have destroyed 100,000,000 other "sane" men in the last 50 years. This fact alone should suffice to reject definitions of normality in which self is modeled after the social order.

In reading Laing, one can learn much about that which mystifies experience and that which amplifies experience. Love and affection mystify experience such that by the time a new human being is 15 years old or so, ". . . we are left with a being like ourselves, a half-crazed creature more or less adjusted to a mad world." Laing's point here is that love is used to reduce one's ability to experience an absurdly few categories out of the whole range of experience.

Positivism mystifies experience in that it requires one to experience things in the pseudo-scientific mode, objectivity. Personal events are experiential; to choose terms and syntax which objectify them is a political act that defines and distorts the human character of these events. The feedback deriving from science further maims and mutilates our children. The product of the mysti-fication process, as Laing puts it, is a child crippled in order to fit into society much as beggars crippled their children to make them fit for a life of begging. Children are betrayed into surrender of self by means of love. They do not easily give up imagination, curiosity, and dreaminess. Love is a betrayal funnel by which we take the child from permissiveness to discipline and then to acceptance, and from acceptance to compliance. And compliance to a schizophrenic social order is betrayal of self.

We have been given by Laing to understand the politics of false experience: politics which removes the joy, the passion, and the meaning from experience. The political tools invoked have been invoked in the name of profit, of progress, of rationality, and in the name of patriotism. It remains with us to develop the *political* tools by which to gain and regain experience. Without experience we cannot exist. With the limits of experience set by the profit and growth curve of large-scale establishments, we can only experience in constricted arenas and constricted modalities. With the experience of students limited to that which facilitates appropriations in a state legislature or with the experience of professors limited to that which polishes the public image of the college, experience in the great issues and causes is foreclosed. When this one example extends across the ranges of the yellow-page society, we are foreclosed as humans.

The real politics of experience is to engage in the same political activity which has been monopolized by naïve parents and teachers and by less than naïve managers. This political activity includes confrontations with those who police experience, those who legislate experience, those who judge experience, and those who serve as ideologues in justification of nonexperience. It means confrontations with the legions of teachers, psychologists, advisers, guidance specialists, personnel managers, social workers, student service personnel, and psychiatrists. A vast army with many legions who use the weapons of understanding, office, and interest in order to lead young people into self-betrayal at just those times when the young are particularly vulnerable.

If many of these functionaries are confronted, then some of them will defect to the cause of selfhood. There is much wisdom and talent together with genuine concern for humanity among psychologists, teachers, and student service personnel. They also have been subjected to the mystification process and fully believe that what they define as "service" is of benefit to our children. When the term "service" is demystified, it emerges as denial of experience and betrayal of self. It is the purpose of this book to demystify the rhetoric of social psychology, self-development and self-presentation, and force the behavioral scientists and practitioners to confront themselves and their own experience. If this purpose is successful, the case of selfhood is advanced.

REFERENCES

Allport, G. W. *Pattern and growth in personality.* New York: Holt, Rinehart & Winston, 1961.

Bach, G. R. The marathon group: Intensive practice of intimate interaction, in *Psychological Reports*, 1966, **18**, 995–1002.

Bach, G. R. Marathon group dynamics: II. Dimensions of helpfulness: Therapeutic aggression. *Psychological Reports*, 1967 b, **20**, 1147–1158.

Bach, G. R. Marathon group dynamics: III. Disjunction contacts. *Psychological Reports*, 1967 c, **20**, 1163–1172.

Baker & Sheldon. *Post-war America: The search for identity.* Beverly Hills: Glencoe Press, 1969.

Baldwin, J. *The child and the rose,* New York: MacMillan, 1895.

Bennis, W. & Slater, P. *The temporary society.* New York: Harper, 1968.

Berger, P. L. & Neuhaus, R. J. *Movement and revolution.* Garden City: Doubleday Anchor, 1970.

Blumer, H. *Symbolic interactionism.* Englewood Cliffs: Prentice-Hall, 1969.

Boorstin, Daniel J. *The image.* New York: Atheneum Press, 1962.

Boskin, J. *Urban racial violence in the twentieth century.* Beverly Hills: Glencoe Press, 1969.

Bottomore, T. B. *Karl Marx: Selected writings in sociology and social philosophy.* New York: McGraw-Hill, 1964.

Bronfenbrenner, U. *Two worlds of childhood: U.S. and U.S.S.R.* Russell Sage Foundation, 1969.

Brown, N. O. *Love's body.* New York: Random House, 1966.

Brown, N. O. *Life against death: The psycho-analytic meaning of history.* Middleton: Wesleyan University Press, 1959.

Brzezinski, Z. The technetronic society. *Encounter*, Jan. 68, Vol. XXX, No. 1, 19.

Buckley, W. *Sociology and modern systems theory.* Englewood Cliffs: Prentice-Hall, 1967.

Burke, K. *A rhetoric of motives.* Englewood Cliffs: Prentice-Hall, 1950.

Cantril, H. *The pattern of human concerns.* New Brunswick, N.J.: Rutgers University Press, 1965.

Casteneda, C. *The teachings of Don Juan.* New York: Ballantine, 1968.

Chai, Ch'u. (Ed.) *I Ching: Book of changes.* Tr. James Legge. New York: Bantam, 1964.

Chinoy, E. *Society: An introduction to sociology.* New York, Random House, 1961.

Cloward, R. Illegitimate means, anomie, and deviant behavior. *ASR*, April 1959, **24**, 164–176.

Cooley, C. H. *Human nature and the social order.* New York: Scribner's, 1902.

Cumming, E. & Henry, W. *Growing old: The process of disengagement.* New York: Basic Books, 1961.

Cuzzort, R. *Humanity & modern sociological thoughts.* New York: Holt, Rinehart & Winston Inc., 1968.

De Levita, D. J. *The concept of identity.* New York: Basic Books, 1965.

Dewey, J. *Experience and education.* New York: Collier, 1963.

Dichter, *Handbook of consumer motivations.* New York: McGraw-Hill, 1964.

Diggory, J. *Self evaluation: Concepts and studies.* New York: Wiley, 1966.

Dostoyevsky, F. *The house of the dead.* New York: Dell, 1959.

Douglas, J. (Ed.) *Freedom and tyranny.* New York: Knopf, 1970.

Duncan, H. D. *Communication and social order.* London: Oxford Press, 1962.

Durkheim, E. *The division of labor in society.* New York: Free Press, 1964.
Durkheim, E. *Suicide.* Tr. J. Simpson. New York: Free Press, 1951.
Easton, D. *Post-behavioral revolution.* 1969.
Eisenstadt, S. N. *From generation to generation.* New York: Free Press, 1956.
Ellul, J. *The technological society.* Tr. J. Wilkenson. New York: Knopf, 1964.
Fenner, R. H. Personal communication, 1967. Cited by R. G. Weigel, Outcomes of marathon group therapy and marathon group topical discussion. Unpublished doctoral dissertation, University of Missouri, 1968.
Fenner, R. H. The use of the marathon for training graduate students in counseling and education: In R. G. Weigel (Chm.), Uses of marathon group counseling in the university setting. Presented at the American Personnel and Guidance Association, Detroit, April 1968.
Fromm, E. *The revolution of hope.* New York: Harper & Row, 1968.
Fromm, E. *The sane society.* New York: Rinehart, 1955.
Gagnon, J. H. & Simon, W. *The sexual scene.* Chicago: Aldine, 1970.
Garfinkel, H. Successful degradation ceremonies, *American Journal of Sociology*, 1956, **61,** 420–424.
Garfinkel, H. *Ethno-methodology.* Englewood Cliffs: Prentice-Hall, 1967.
Goffman, E. *Stigma.* Englewood Cliffs: Prentice-Hall, 1963.
Goffman, E. *Interaction ritual.* Chicago: Aldine, 1967.
Goffman, E. *Asylums.* Garden City: Anchor, 1961a.
Goffman, E. *Encounters.* Indianapolis: Bobbs-Merril, 1961b.
Goffman, E. *Behavior in public places.* New York: Free Press, 1963.
Goffman, E. *The presentation of self in everyday life.* Garden City: Doubleday Anchor, 1959.
Goldenweiser, A. In Barnes & Becker, *Contemporary social theory.* New York: Appleton-Century, 1940.
Goodman, P. *The empire city.* New York: Macmillan, 1964.
Goodman, P. *Growing up absurd.* New York: Random House, 1960.
Gouldner, Alvin W. *The coming crisis of western sociology.* New York: Basic Books, 1970.
Grant, L. *Astrology for the millions.* New York: 1940.
Hall, C. S. & Lindsey, G. *Theories of personality.* New York: Wiley, 1957.
Hetzler, S. *Technological growth and social change.* London: Routledge & Kegan Paul, 1969.
Hughes, E. C. *Men and their work.* New York: Free Press, 1958.
Hurst, J. & Uhlemann, M. Personal communication.
Josephson, E. & Josephson, M. *Man alone: Alienation in modern society.* New York: Dell, 1962.
Koffka, K. *Principles of gestalt psychology.* New York: Harcourt Brace, & World, 1935.
Kohler, W. *Gestalt psychology.* New York: Liveright, 1929.
Knop, E. C. *Timbertown in transition.* Unpublished dissertation, University of Minnesota 1969.
Kuhn, M. H. & McPartland, T. S. An empirical investigation of self attitudes. *American Sociological Review*, 1954, **19,** 68–76.
Laing, R. O. *The politics of experience.* New York: Ballantine, 1967.
Lasswell, T., Burma, J. H. & Aronson, S. H. *Life in society.* Chicago: Scott, Foresman, 1965.
Levi, Grant. *Astrology for the millions*: Garden City: Doubleday Doran, 1942.

Lewin, K. *Dynamic theory of personality*. New York: McGraw-Hill, 1935.
Lincoln, C. E. *The black Muslims in America*. Boston: Beacon Press, 1961.
Manis, J. G. & Meltzer, B. N. *Symbolic interaction*. Boston: Allyn & Bacon, 1967.
Mannheim, K. *Ideology and Utopia*. New York: Harvest Books, 1936.
Marcuse, H. *Eros and civilization*. New York: Vintage, 1962.
Marcuse, H. *One-dimensional man*. Boston: Beacon Press, 1964
Marcuson, S. (Ed.) *Automation, alienation and anomie*. New York: Harper & Row, 1970.
Martindale, D. *The nature and types of sociological theory*. Boston: Houghton-Mifflin, 1960.
Marx, Karl. *Economic and philosophical manuscript*. 1844.
Maslow, A. H. *New knowledge in human values*. New York: Harper & Brothers, 1959.
Maslow, A. H. *Toward a psychology of being*. Princeton: Van Nostrand, 1962.
May, R. (Ed.) *Existential psychology*. New York: Random House, 1961.
McLuhan, M. *Understanding media*. New York: McGraw-Hill, 1964.
Mead, G. H. *Mind, self, and society*. Chicago: University of Chicago Press, 1934.
Merrill, F. E. *Society & culture*. Englewood Cliffs: Prentice-Hall, 1961.
Merton, R. K. Social structure and anomie. *ASR*, Oct. 1938, **3**, 672–682.
Mintz, E. E. Time-extended marathon groups. *Psycho-Therapy: Theory, Research, and Practice*, 1967, **4** (2), 65–70.
Natanson, M. *The journeying self*. Reading: Addison-Wesley, 1970.
Naylor, P. I. H. *Astrology: An historical examination*. London: Maxwell, 1967.
Nisbet, R. A. *Emile Durkheim*. Englewood Cliffs: Prentice-Hall, 1965.
Piaget, J. *Dreams and imitations in childhood*. New York: Norton, 1962.
Poppenheim, F. *The alienation of modern man*. New York: Modern Reader, 1959.
Psychology Today, Del Mar, California: CRM, August, 1970.
Psychology Today. Del Mar, California: CRM, February, 1971.
Putney, Snell & Gail. *The adjusted American: Normal neuroses in the individual and society*. New York: Harper & Row, 1964.
Rainwater, L. *Soul: Black experience*. Chicago: Aldine, 1970.
Reich, C. A. The greening of America. *The New Yorker*, Sept. 26, 1970: 42–111.
Riesman, D. *The lonely crowd*. New Haven: Yale University Press, 1950.
Rogers, C. R. *On becoming a person*. Boston: Houghton-Mifflin, 1961.
Roszak, T. *The making of a counter culture*. Garden City: Doubleday Anchor, 1969.
Sargent, S. S. & Williamson, R. C. *Social psychology*. New York: Ronald Press, 1966.
Sherif, M. & Sherif, C. W. *Social psychology*. New York: Harper & Row, 1969.
Snygg, D. & Combs, A. W. *Individual behavior*. New York: Harper, 1949.
Sorokin, P. A. *Society, culture, and personality*. New York: Cooper Square Publishers, 1942.
Stein, M. & Miller, L. *Blueprints for counter education*. New York: Doubleday.
Stoller, F. H. *Marathon group therapy*. Unpublished manuscript, 1967a.
Stoller, F. H. The long weekend. *Psychology Today*, 1967b, **1**, 28–33.
Sullivan, H. S. Beginnings of the self-system. In Ullman, A. D. (Ed.), *Sociocultural foundations of personality*. Boston: Houghton-Mifflin, 1965. Pp. 141–146.
Szasz, T. *The myth of mental illness*. New York: Hoeber-Harper, 1961.
Szasz, T. *Ideology and insanity*. Garden City: Doubleday Anchor, 1970.
Uhlemann, M. R. Behavioral change outcomes and marathon group therapy. Unpublished M. S. thesis, C.S.U., 1968.
Ungerer, P. D. (Ed.) Existential psychiatry: *Journal of the American Ontological Society* Seven Bridges, Chicago, Vol. 7, No. 26–27.

Van den Haag, E. Of happiness and despair we have no measure. In *Mass Culture*. New York: Rosenberg and White, (Eds.) Free Press, 1957.

Van Gennep, A. *Rites of passage*. Chicago: University of Chicago Press, 1966.

Van Kaam, A. *Existential foundations of psychology*. New York: Doubleday Image, 1969.

Veblen, T. *The higher learning in America*. New York: Hill & Wang, 1962.

Wagstaff, T. *Black power*. Beverly Hills: Glencoe Press, 1969.

Wakefield, D. *Supernation at peace and war*. Boston: Bantam, 1968.

Weigel, R. G. Marathon group therapy and marathon group discussion. A paper presented at the American Personnel and Guidance Association, Las Vegas, 1968.

Wheeler, L. *Interpersonal influence*. Boston: Allyn & Bacon, 1970.

White, D. M. *Pop culture in America*. Chicago: Quadrangle, 1970.

Whyte, W. F. *The organization man*. New York: Doubleday, 1956.

Wiener, N. *The human use of human beings*. New York: Avon, 1967.

Winick, C. *The new people: Desexualization in America*. New York: Pegasus, 1968.

Wolfe, T. *The kandy kolored tangerine flake streamline baby*. New York: Farrar, 1963.

Wylie, R. C. *The self concept: A critical survey of pertinent research literature*. Lincoln, Nebr.: University of Nebraska Press, 1961.

Yablonsky, L. *The hippie trip*. New York: Pegasus, 1969.

Young, R. & Oberdorfer, D. W. Psychological studies of social process. In Barnes, Becker and Becker (Eds.), *Contemporary Social Theory*. New York: Appleton-Century, 1940. Pp. 337–346, 389.

Young, T. R. Some speculations on the sociology of recreation. Annual Meeting of Missouri State Sociological Society, St. Louis, Mo., 1962.

Young, T. R. The Black Muslims: A strategy for the management of spoiled identity. With Paul Chassy. Cahiers Internationaux de Sociologie, Paris, France, forthcoming.

Young, T. R. Short-takes and Self-Systems. *Rocky Mountain Social Science Association*, Denver, 1968.

Young, T. R. Camp and Corruption. *Rocky Mountain Social Science Association*, Denver, 1968.

Young, T. R. The sociology of classroom teaching: A microfunctional analysis. In collaboration with P. Beardsley. *Journal of Education Thought*, April 1968.

AUTHOR INDEX

Adler, A. 20
Albertus, Magnus 70
Allport, Gordon 73
Anaxagoras 70
Aristotle 70
Avant Garde 104

Bach, G. R. 75
Baldwin, James 1, 44
Baker, Donald G. 30
Bennis, Warren 99
Blumer, Herbert 5, 6, 22
Boorstin, D. J. 54, 55
Boyd, Malcolm 61
Brahe, Tycho 70
Bronfenbrenner U. 35, 36
Brown, Charles 59, 61, 63
Brown, Norman O. 4, 32, 42
Brezinski, Z. 59
Buckley, Walter 14
Burns, Sam 24
Burke, Kenneth 44

Caesar 70
Cagliostro 70
Caligula 70
Cantril, H. 17
Casteneda, Carlos 95
Chaucer 70
Chinoy, E. 52
Cooley, Charles H. ix, 1, 6, 16, 17, 19
Combs, A. W. 20
Cuming, Elaine 86
Cuzzort, Ray 52, 56

Dante 70
Dichter, E. 46
Dixon, Jeanne 71
Dewey, John 2
Don Juan 96, 97
Diggory, J. 20

Domhoff, William 42
Dostoyevsky ix
Durkheim, Emile 15, 29, 30, 91, 97
Easton, David 82
Einstein, Albert 20
Eisenhower, David 86
Eisenstadt, S. N. 24
Erikson, E. 18
Evergreen 104

Fenner, R. H. 75
Flacks, Richard 33
Freud, Sigmund 1, 20, 32, 44
Fromm, Erich x, 4, 41, 42, 73, 83, 89

Gardner, Murphy 21
Garfinkel, Harold 6, 7, 49
Goffman, Erving 6, 7, 8, 18, 19, 49
      52, 53, 56, 89
Golightly, C. 52
Gouldner, A. 52, 55–56

Henry II 70
Henry, W. 86
Hetzler, Stanley 17, 33
Hitler 71
Hurst, James 75

Jeremiah 70
Josephson, E. 27
Josephson, M. 27
John 70
Jung, Carl 20

Kepler, Johannes 70
Kesey, Ken 65
Kissinger, H. 4
Koffka, K. 19
Kohler, W. 19
Knop, Edward 68, 86
Kuhn, Manford 10, 22

111

SUBJECT INDEX

113